SETTING THE RECORD STRAIGHT
JOSEPH SMITH:
PRESIDENTIAL
CANDIDATE

Cover: The images on the cover represent Joseph Smith's candidacy for President of the United States of America. The image on the left is the Presidential Seal of the United States of America. The image on the right is an image of a mature Joseph Smith sharing gospel truths.

SETTING THE RECORD STRAIGHT

JOSEPH SMITH:
PRESIDENTIAL
CANDIDATE

Arnold K. Garr, Ph.D.

Millennial Press, Inc.
P.O. Box 1741
Orem, UT 84059

ISBN: 1-932597-53-0

Cover design and typesetting by Adam Riggs

Contents

Preface

"Great men taken up in any way, are profitable company," observed historian Thomas Carlyle. "We cannot look . . . upon a great man without gaining something [from] him."[1]

From a Latter-day Saint perspective, Joseph Smith was certainly one of the greatest men in history: "The Prophet and Seer of the Lord, has done more, save Jesus only, for the salvation of men in this world, than any other man that ever lived in it" (D&C 135:3).

Hundreds of books and articles have been written about Joseph Smith through the years. Why then do we need another book about the Prophet? While the majority of the books published thus far about him have discussed his tremendous achievements as a spiritual leader, this book endeavors to tell the story of his remarkable accomplishments as a governmental leader.

The fact that Joseph Smith was such a giant of a man spiritually has unfortunately overshadowed the reality that he was also a skilled statesman who was heavily involved in politics during the last five years of his life. From 1839 to 1844 he visited with the president of the United States, helped draft the Nauvoo Charter, and served diligently and effectively as a city councilor, vice mayor, and mayor of Nauvoo. Of course, during the last five months of his life, he also ran for president of the United States.

The purpose of this book is to tell the story of Joseph Smith's political activities, with emphasis on his campaign for president. This book is the culmination of thirteen years of researching and writing on the subject. Since 1995 I have published six articles on the political life of the Prophet.[2]

I am grateful to the many people who have helped me on this project. Thanks to Richard M. Turley Jr., executive director of the Latter-day Saint Family and Church History Department in Salt Lake City. He allowed me access to all of the Nauvoo City Council minutes. These minutes were an extremely important source of information for the chapters, which discuss the activities of Joseph Smith as a city councilor and mayor.

I would like to thank Linda Godfrey, secretary of the Department of Church History and Doctrine. She made the part-time student receptionists available to me to work on this volume. These four capable young ladies—Michelle Cameron, Meara Glazebrook, Kylee Pearson, and Ariel Wood—faithfully helped me type, check sources, and proofread the manuscript.

I am grateful to Randy Bott for encouraging me to publish this book with Millennial Press. Thanks to Ryan Bott for skillfully and expeditiously orchestrating the entire publication process. He has been a joy to work with. I also appreciate the fine work of Lindsey Shumway.

I would especially like to thank my wife, Cherie, who has always demonstrated remarkable kindness, patience, and understanding when I have been involved in writing or editing books. Finally, I would like to express my appreciation to my mother, Lucile Garr, who is in her 100th year. She has always given me love and encouragement.

Chronology of Joseph Smith's Political Activities

1839

March: Received a revelation to gather statements and affidavits that detailed the abuses suffered by the Saints at the hands of the people of Missouri. These affidavits (petitions for redress) were to be presented to the heads of government (see D&C 123:1–6).

October 20:   The Nauvoo High Council votes that Joseph Smith go to Washington, D.C., and present Church grievances to President Martin Van Buren.

November 29:   Joseph Smith meets with President Van Buren.

1840

February 6:   The Prophet meets with President Van Buren a second time.*

October 4:   During general conference, Joseph Smith, John C. Bennett, and Robert B. Thompson are appointed to draft the Nauvoo Charter.

December 16:   The Illinois Legislature approves the Nauvoo Charter.

1841

February 1:   Joseph Smith is elected as one of the original members of the Nauvoo City Council.

1842

January 22:   Joseph Smith is elected vice mayor of Nauvoo.

May 19:   The Prophet is elected mayor of Nauvoo.

1843

November 4:   Joseph Smith writes letters to the five leading candidates for president of the United States.

1844

January 29:   Joseph Smith announces that he will run for president of the United States.

February 7:   The Prophet completes and signs *General Smith's Views of the Powers and Policy of the Government of the United States*.

February 24:   1,500 copies of *General Smith's Views* are printed.

February 27:   *General Smith's Views* are sent to the president of the United States and his cabinet, justices of the Supreme Court, senators, representatives, postmasters, and principal newspapers. At least forty-five newspapers in twenty-two of the twenty-six states publish articles about Joseph Smith's campaign.

March 11:   The Council of Fifty is organized.

April 9:   In general conference, 244 people volunteer to be electioneer missionaries.

April 15:   The Twelve Apostles appoint 337 electioneer missionaries to serve in all twenty-six states and in the Wisconsin Territory. They also arrange for forty-seven conferences in fifteen different states.

May 17:   A state convention is held for Joseph Smith in Nauvoo.

June 10:   As mayor, Joseph Smith orders the city marshal to destroy the press of the *Nauvoo Expositor*.

June 18:   The Prophet puts Nauvoo under marital law and mobilizes the Nauvoo Legion and the municipal police.

June 24:   Joseph Smith reluctantly countersigns a bill with Gov. Thomas Ford that disarms the Nauvoo Legion.

June 25:   Joseph Smith voluntarily goes to jail in Carthage.

June 27:   The Prophet is martyred.

July 1:   A state convention is held for Joseph Smith in Boston. (Those attending did not know the Prophet had been killed.)

* Some scholars believe that the February 6, 1840, meeting with President Van Buren (Smith, *History of the Church*, 4:80) was simply a retelling of the meeting held November 29, 1839 (Smith, *History of the Church*, 4:40).

Frequently Asked Questions about the Political activities of Joseph Smith

1. Why did Joseph Smith meet with President Martin Van Buren?

After the Saints had been expelled from the state of Missouri in 1838, Joseph Smith received a revelation while he was imprisoned in the Liberty Jail (D&C 123). The revelation stated that the Church should appeal its case to the "heads of government" in order to get compensation for the mistreatment of the Saints. The revelation admonished members of the Church to "gather up knowledge of all facts, and sufferings and abuses put upon them by the people of this State [of Missouri]" (D&C 123:1). These facts were recorded in the form of affidavits known as

Liberty Jail is where Joseph Smith received a revelation that the Church should appeal its case to the heads of government (D&C 123:1-6). They were to gather up knowledge of all the facts and the sufferings and the abuses put upon them by the people of Missouri. These became known as petitions for redress.

petitions for redress.[3] On October 20, 1839, the Nauvoo High Council voted that Joseph Smith go as a delegate to Washington, D.C., and present the Church's grievances to the president and Congress.[4] The Prophet met with President Van Buren in response to this request.

2. How did President Van Buren respond to Joseph Smith's request?

According to the Prophet, Van Buren treated him rudely and declared: "Gentlemen, your cause is just, but I can do nothing for you. . . . If I take up for you I shall lose the vote of Missouri."[5]

3. Did Joseph Smith have any interaction with the leading presidential candidates in 1844?

Yes. On November 4, 1843, Joseph Smith wrote letters to John C. Calhoun, Lewis Cass, Richard M. Johnson, Henry Clay, and Martin Van Buren, the five leading candidates for the presidency of the United States. Each letter talked of the persecutions the Latter-day Saints suffered at the hands of the state of Missouri and then asked a pointed question: "What will be your rule of action relative to us as a people, should fortune favor your ascension to the chief magistracy?"[6]

Martin Van Buren

Van Buren and Johnson never responded to Joseph Smith's letters. Calhoun, Cass, and Clay did respond, but they were unwilling to pledge their support to the Church. Therefore, Joseph Smith began to consider running for president himself.

4. When did Joseph Smith decide to run for president of the United States?

When he determined that none of the leading candidates for president would pledge support in helping the Saints gain redress, the Prophet held a historic meeting in the mayor's office in Nauvoo on January 29, 1844. During that meeting, which was attended by the Quorum of the Twelve Apostles and other leaders, Willard Richards made a motion that Joseph Smith should run for the presidency on an independent electoral ticket and that those present should use "all honorable means in [their] power to secure his election."[7]

5. Why did Joseph Smith decide to run for president?

Joseph Smith's primary motivation for running for president of the United States was to do all in his power to protect the Latter-day Saints from the kinds of injustices they had suffered in Missouri. On February 8, 1844, the Prophet declared:

"I would not have suffered my name to have been used by my friends on anywise as President of the United States, or candidate for that office, if I and my friends could have had the privilege of enjoying our religious and civil rights as American citizens, even those rights which the Constitution guarantees unto all her citizens alike. But this as a people we have been denied from the beginning. Persecution has rolled upon our heads from time to time, from portions of the Untied States, like peals of thunder, because of our religion; and no portion of this government as yet has stepped forward for our relief. And in view of these things, I feel it to be my right and privilege to obtain what influence and power I can, lawfully, in the United States, for the protection of injured innocence."[8]

6. How much experience did Joseph Smith have in government before he ran for president?

He had met with President Van Buren and several members of the U.S. Congress in the winter of 1839–40. He helped draft the Nauvoo Charter. He was elected one of the original members of the Nauvoo City Council on February 1, 1841. He was elected mayor of Nauvoo on May 19, 1842.

7. What was Joseph Smith's presidential platform?

On January 29, 1844, the Prophet met with William W. Phelps and dictated to him the headings for a pamphlet titled *General Smith's Views of the Powers and Policy of the Government of the United States.*[9] This pamphlet became the foundation for his presidential platform. Joseph advocated giving power to the president to suppress mobs. He also favored abolishing slavery, reducing both the number and pay of the House of Representatives, reforming the prison system, eliminating courts-martial for desertion, forming a national bank, and annexing Oregon and Texas.

8. How widely was *General Smith's Views of the Powers and Policy of the Government of the United States* circulated?

On February 24, he had 1,500 copies of *Views* printed.[10] Three days later he had copies mailed to the president of the United States and his cabinet, the justices of the Supreme Court, "senators, representatives, principal newspapers in the United States, . . . and many postmasters."[11]

9. What were the two major political parties in 1844?

Democrats and Whigs.

10. What political party did Joseph Smith align himself with?

Joseph Smith was a third-party candidate. The name of his party was Reformed Jeffersonian Democracy, Free Trade and Sailors Rights.[12]

11. Who was Joseph Smith's vice-presidential running mate?

Sidney Rigdon, first counselor in the First Presidency of the Church.[13]

Sidney Rigdon

12. Who organized and supervised Joseph Smith's presidential campaign?

Brigham Young and the Quorum of the Twelve Apostles.[14] All of the members of the Quorum of the Twelve were also members of an organization called the Council of Fifty, "a political entity outside the regular organization of the Church although dominated by priesthood leaders."[15] The Council of Fifty was given "some practical responsibilities for organizing Joseph Smith's presidential campaign."[16] Because all of the Apostles were members of both the Quorum of the Twelve and the Council of Fifty, "the distinction between the political and ecclesiastical kingdoms blurred."[17]

13. What was Joseph Smith's campaign strategy?

When, during the April 1844 general conference, the Quorum of the Twelve called for volunteers to serve political/religious missions, 244 people stepped forward.[18] Thus began something unique in American as well as Mormon history—missionaries called to campaign for their presidential candidate and simultaneously proselytize for their church.

During the next few days, additional missionaries were called, bringing the total to at least 337.[19] On April 15 these missionaries were assigned to all twenty-six states in the Union, as well as the Wisconsin Territory. The state of New York was assigned the most missionaries (forty-seven), while the Wisconsin Territory received the fewest (one).[20] The Apostles also designated one or two elders to preside over the missionaries of each state.[21] The Quorum of the Twelve scheduled a series of forty-seven conferences to be held in fifteen states and the nation's capital, starting in Quincy, Illinois, on May 4 and ending in Washington, D.C., on September 15.[22]

14. Did the members of the Quorum of the Twelve campaign for Joseph Smith?

Yes, most members of the Quorum of the Twelve campaigned for the Prophet throughout the eastern United States, especially in New England.

15. How much publicity did the newspapers give to Joseph Smith's campaign?

At least forty-five newspapers located in twenty-two states published articles concerning *General Smith's Views*.[23] Obviously, the newspapers printed mixed responses, but many were favorable.[24]

16. Did Joseph Smith receive any revelations concerning politics?

Not that we know of. The Prophet once declared: "The Lord has not given me a revelation concerning politics. I have not asked him for one. I am a third party, and stand independent and alone."[25]

17. How serious was Joseph Smith's campaign for president?

On January 29, 1844, the Prophet declared, "If I ever get into the presidential chair, I will protect the people in their rights and liberties. . . . There is oratory enough in the Church to carry me into the presidential chair the first slide."[26] On February 7, he said, "I feel it to be my right and privilege to obtain what influence and power I can, lawfully, in the United States for the protection of injured innocence."[27] Joseph then went on to speculate that he might be killed because of the campaign. These are hardly the words of a frivolous candidate.

Nevertheless, B. H. Roberts did not consider the Prophet a serious candidate. "Of course President Smith could have no hope that he would be elected to the presidency," he said, adding that the Prophet "usually referred to his candidacy in a jocular vein."[28] Roberts justified his position by quoting the following statement from the Prophet: "I care but little about the presidential chair. I would not give half as much for the office of President of the United States as I would for . . . Lieutenant-General of the Nauvoo Legion."[29]

In an article published in the *Ensign* magazine in 1973, author James B. Allen acknowledged that the seriousness of Joseph Smith's campaign is "still a matter of debate even among Church historians."[30] He cautions readers against taking "dogmatic" positions that "are based on circumstantial evidence and subjective reasoning."[31] Allen's opinion is that while the Prophet did not think he could win the presidency, "he was serious in attempting to influence public opinion by using every possible means to promote his own political views."[32]

It would seem, therefore, that if the Prophet directed Church leaders to call more than three hundred men to campaign in every state of the Union and organize forty-seven conferences in fifteen different states, then he was absolutely serious about influencing public opinion, especially regarding the powers of the president of the United States. The fact that at least forty-five newspapers, located in twenty-two different states, published articles about Joseph Smith's campaign suggests that the Prophet, indeed, had some influence on public opinion. In addition, the fact that so many editors chose to publish articles about his campaign indicates that numerous newspapers took his campaign seriously.

18. How successful was Joseph Smith's campaign?

We have no way of knowing because his campaign was cut short by his martyrdom.

19. Why don't we hear more about Joseph Smith's campaign for president?

Because he was martyred on June 27, 1844—months before the election took place.

20. Who won the presidential election of 1844?

James K. Polk, the Democratic candidate, was elected president. "The actual popular vote stood as follows . . . : James K. Polk, Democrat, 1,337,000; Henry Clay, Whig, 1,299,000; James G. Birney, Liberty (Abolitionist) Party, 62,000." Polk received 170 electoral votes, Clay received 105, and Birney received none.[33]

Joseph Smith Meets President Van Buren: A Turning Point

"The Mormons must be treated as enemies and *must be exterminated* or driven from the state," proclaimed Missouri governor Lilburn W. Boggs on October 27, 1838. "Their outrages are beyond all description."[34]

This shameful extermination order is perhaps the most infamous statement in the history of the Latter-day Saints.[35] The governor issued this decree after apostates and Mormon haters had given him distorted and exaggerated reports that accused the Latter-day Saints of insurrection. Ignoring any information he might have received concerning the Mormon point of view, Boggs was led to believe that the Latter-day Saints were making "open war upon the people" of Missouri.[36]

The governor commissioned the state militia to carry out the extermination order. Within the next three days, approximately 2,500 troops had converged on the Latter-day Saint community of Far West, calling for the Mormons to surrender. By October 31, 1838, the Saints submitted to the demands of the militia and agreed to leave Missouri.[37] As a result, approximately ten thousand Saints were forced to evacuate the state and seek refuge in Illinois during the winter and spring of 1838–39.[38] This tragic extermination order also served as the catalyst that thrust the Prophet Joseph Smith into politics for the rest of his life.

In the midst of this heart-wrenching exodus, the leaders of

the Church discussed ways in which the Saints might obtain redress for the property lost and afflictions suffered during the Missouri persecutions. In March 1839, while imprisoned in Liberty Jail, Joseph Smith received a revelation that said the Church should appeal its case to the "heads of government" in order to get compensation for the mistreatment of the Saints. The revelation admonished members of the Church to "gather up knowledge of all the facts, and sufferings and abuses put upon them by the people of this State" of Missouri (D&C 123:1). These facts were recorded in the form of sworn affidavits known as petitions for redress.[39]

Seven months later, on October 20, 1839, the Nauvoo High Council voted that Joseph Smith go as a delegate to Washington, D.C., and present the Church's grievances to the president and Congress. By October 28, Sidney Rigdon and Elias Higbee had received appointments to accompany the Prophet.[40] Orrin Porter Rockwell served as a driver for the delegates.

The Road to Washington, D.C.

These four men left Nauvoo, Illinois, in a two-horse carriage on Tuesday, October 29, 1839, and traveled to Quincy, Illinois, where Sidney Rigdon became ill. Between Quincy and Springfield, Illinois, Robert Foster, a medical doctor, joined them in order to care for ailing President Rigdon.[41] The party arrived in Springfield, the state capital, on Monday, November 4.

Joseph Smith and his companions remained in Springfield for most of the week, where the Prophet preached on several occasions. One of his listeners was Gen. James Adams, a county probate judge, who invited Joseph Smith to his home and reportedly treated the Prophet as if he were his own son.[42] Judge Adams also wrote a letter of recommendation to President Martin Van Buren in behalf of Joseph Smith and the other delegates.[43]

While staying in Springfield, the Prophet wrote a touching letter to his wife, Emma. The correspondence gives insight into the private life of the Prophet and his willingness to sacrifice time with his family in order to help the cause of the Church. In the letter Joseph spoke of the "constant anxiety" he felt for his wife and children. It was especially painful for him to leave his three-year-old son, Frederick, who was sick at the time of his departure. The Prophet lamented:

"It will be a long and lonesome time during my absence from you and nothing but a sense of humanity could have urged me on to so great a sacrifice, but shall I see so many perish and [not] seek redress? No, I will try this once in the [name] of the Lord. Therefore be patient."[44]

Joseph Smith and his party left Springfield on, or shortly after, November 8, 1839. It took them about ten days to get to Columbus, Ohio. By this time Sidney Rigdon had become too sick to travel any farther. Under these circumstances the Prophet thought it best to leave President Rigdon in Columbus under the care of Dr. Foster until the former regained his health. Orrin Porter Rockwell stayed with them. Joseph Smith and Elias Higbee then continued their journey to Washington, D.C., by stagecoach.[45]

During the last phase of the trip, Joseph Smith became involved in an act of bravery that was as exciting as a scene from an action-packed, old-time cowboy movie. As the Prophet's party approached Washington, D.C., the driver stopped the stage and went into a "public house" to get a drink. While the coachman was having his "grog," the horses became frightened and "ran down the hill at full speed." The passengers became terrified, and some started to panic. One lady became so hysterical that she attempted to throw her baby out of the window.

Joseph Smith did all he could to get the passengers to calm their nerves and stay in their seats. Then he performed a remarkable act of courage. He opened the door of the stage and climbed up the side of the coach until he made his way to the driver's seat. He somehow got hold of the reins and brought the horses to a halt, "after they had run some two or three miles."

The passengers, all uninjured, were most grateful, calling Joseph Smith's deed "daring and heroic." Some of them, members of Congress, proposed the idea of mentioning the Prophet's act of bravery in a session of Congress, "believing they would reward such conduct by some public act." However, when the congressmen found out that their hero was Joseph Smith, "the Mormon Prophet," their enthusiasm quickly diminished. "I heard no more of their praise, gratitude or reward," said the Prophet.[46]

The Prophet Meets the President

Joseph Smith and Elias Higbee finally arrived in the nation's capital on Thursday, November 28, 1839. They stayed in an inexpensive boarding house on the corner of Missouri and Third Streets. Joseph said it was "as cheap a place as can be had in this city."[47]

The next morning they walked up to the door of the White House and requested an audience with President Van Buren. They were ushered into the parlor, where they were introduced to the president. They gave Van Buren their letters of recommendation, but after reading one of them, the president frowned and declared, "What can I do? I can do nothing for you! If I do anything I shall

The White House

come in contact with the whole state of Missouri."[48]

After further discussion, however, Van Buren promised to reconsider his position and "felt to sympathize with [the Mormons], on account of [their] suffering."[49]

During the course of the interview, the men also discussed religion. President Van Buren asked how Mormonism differed "from other religions of the day." Joseph Smith replied, "We differ in the method of baptism and the gift of the Holy Ghost by the laying on of hands." The Prophet then recorded, "We deemed it unnecessary to make many words in preaching the Gospel to him. Suffice it to say he has got our testimony."[50]

After their visit with the president, the Prophet and Elias Higbee met with several senators and representatives who might be willing to espouse their cause. On December 6, they began a series of meetings with the congressional delegation from Illinois, which was especially helpful. After some discussion, it was decided that the congressmen from Illinois would draw up a memorial and petition and that Richard P. Young, a U.S. senator from Illinois, would present the document to the Senate.[51]

The lengthy petition, which is reproduced in the *History of the Church,* is fourteen single-spaced pages long. It enumerated the persecutions the Saints had endured in Missouri since being expelled from Jackson County in 1833. The document concluded with an impassioned plea: "For ourselves we see no redress, unless it is awarded by the Congress of the United States. And here we make our appeal as *American Citizens*, as *Christians*, and as *Men*—believing that the high sense of justice that exists in your honorable body, will not allow such oppression to be practiced on any portion of the citizens of this vast republic with impunity."[52]

Senator Young faithfully introduced the petition in the Senate, which, in turn, referred it to the Judiciary Committee.[53] In the meantime, Joseph Smith and Elias Higbee wrote to the Saints in Illinois, asking them to send as many sworn affidavits as possible that would specifically confirm their persecutions and property lost in Missouri.[54] Altogether the Mormon delegates submitted 491 individual petitions for redress to Congress. These petitions itemized claims against the state of Missouri that amounted to $1,381,044.[55]

While Joseph Smith was in the East, he also took the opportunity to do what he loved most—preach the gospel and visit the branches of the Church. On December 21, 1839, he took a train to Philadelphia, where he "spent several days preaching and visiting from house to house."[56]

Elder Parley P. Pratt, who was staying in Philadelphia at the time, wrote about how much he enjoyed spending time with the Prophet: "It was at this time that I received from him the first idea of eternal family organization. . . . It was from him that I learned that the wife of my bosom might be sealed to me for time and all eternity."[57]

Elder Pratt also told of an occasion when Joseph Smith spoke to a crowd of three thousand people who had assembled in a large church in Philadelphia: "Joseph rose like a lion about to roar; and being full of the Holy Ghost, spoke in great power, bearing testimony of the visions he had seen, the ministering of angels which he had enjoyed; and how he had found the plates of the Book of Mormon, and translated them by the gift and power of God." Elder Pratt added, "The entire congregation was astonished; electrified as it were, and overwhelmed with the sense of the truth and power by which he spoke, and the wonders which he related. . . . Many souls were gathered into the fold."[58]

At the end of January 1840, the Prophet returned to Washington, D.C., where he continued to preach the gospel.[59] He gave a two-hour sermon on the evening of February 5, 1840, which was attended by U.S. Congressman Matthew S. Davis. Davis wrote a letter to his wife, Mary, describing in detail the Prophet's sermon. He explained that Mormonism "appears to be the religion of meekness, lowliness and mild persuasion." He concluded his letter by saying, *"I have changed my opinion of the Mormons.* They are an injured and much abused people."[60]

Soon after Joseph Smith's return to the nation's capital, he had another interview with President Van Buren, who by this time had lost any sympathetic feelings he might have had for the Church.[61] According to the Prophet, Van Buren treated him rudely and declared, "Gentlemen, your cause is just, but I can do nothing for you. . . . If I take up for you I shall lose the vote of Missouri."[62]

Frustrated and disappointed with the President, Joseph Smith complained that Van Buren's "whole course went to show that he was an office seeker, that self-aggrandizement was his ruling passion, and that justice and righteousness were no part of his composition." The Prophet felt that he could no longer "conscientiously support" such a man at the head of the government. Joseph now believed that it was no longer beneficial for him to stay in Washington, and he departed for Nauvoo on or before February 20.[63]

The Prophet was so infuriated with the president that he declared, "On my way home I did not fail to proclaim the iniquity and insolence of Martin Van Buren, toward myself and an injured people . . . and may he never be elected again to any office of trust or power, by which he may abuse the innocent and let the guilty go free." Joseph Smith's wish came true. Martin Van Buren lost the election of 1840 to William Henry Harrison, the Whig candidate. In 1848, when Van Buren ran again for president, this time as a candidate for the Free Soil Party, he "did not receive a single electoral vote."[64]

When the Prophet left for Nauvoo, Elias Higbee stayed behind to work with the Senate Judiciary Committee on the petition. Between February 20 and March 24, Higbee wrote six letters to the Prophet, informing him of the activities of the Senate.[65] On March 4, the Judiciary Committee submitted its formal report to the twenty-sixth Congress. The committee, in response, simply washed its hands of any jurisdiction or responsibility in the case, declaring, "The committee, under these circumstances, have not considered themselves justified in inquiring into the truth or falsehood of the facts charged in the petition." In its report, the committee had the audacity to recommend that the Church "apply to the justice and magnanimity of the state of Missouri." Finally it recommended "that the committee on the judiciary be discharged from further consideration of the memorial in this case."[66]

On March 24, Elias Higbee sadly reported, "Our business is at last ended here. Yesterday a resolution passed the Senate, that the committee should be discharged; and that we might withdraw the accompanying papers, which I have done. I have also taken a copy of the memorial, and want to be off for the west immediately." Though their work ended in disappointment, Higbee seemed to be at peace with the fact that he gave it his best effort. He concluded, "But there is no need to cry for spilt milk. I have done all I could in this matter."[67]

On April 7, at the general conference of the Church held in Nauvoo, the Prophet Joseph Smith gave a report on the trip to Washington, D.C. The next day the conference formally thanked the delegates for their efforts in seeking redress for the Saints from the national government. Within the next few months it became clear that the Prophet had lost all confidence that any branch of the federal government would help the Latter-day Saints. On July 19, 1840, he declared, "We will continue pleading like the Widow at the feet of the unjust judge," he remarked, "but we may plead at the feet of Majistrates and at the feet of Judges, at the feet of Governors and at the feet of senators & at the feet of Pre[s]idents for 8 years [but] it will be of no avail." Then the Prophet exclaimed, "We shall find no favor in any of the courts of this government."[68]

Joseph Smith Becomes a Member of the Nauvoo City Council

The experience in the nation's capital led the Prophet to take a more active role in politics. Thereafter he became an energetic participant in local, state, and national politics—hoping that his own involvement and political influence might be the means of protecting and promoting the cause of his people. However, it was in local politics, particularly in Nauvoo city government, that the Prophet played the most active political role.

The Nauvoo Charter

In late 1840, Joseph Smith and other Church leaders set out to create a municipal form of government with a judicial system designed to provide a safe haven for their people. This effort formally began during the Sunday morning session of the October 1840 general conference of the Church. During that meeting, Joseph Smith, John C. Bennett, and Robert B. Thompson were appointed "to draft a bill for the incorporation of the town of Nauvoo."[69]

John C. Bennett

In a separate resolution, John C. Bennett was nominated to "urge the passage of said bill" through the Illinois State Legislature.[70] Following a one-hour recess between conference sessions, Bennett presented the outlines of the Nauvoo Charter, which members in attendance approved.[71] The fact that this all happened so rapidly seems to suggest that the Prophet, Bennett, and others probably worked on the document informally before the conference even began.[72] The Prophet was deeply involved in the project for good reason. He once declared, "The City Charter of Nauvoo is of my own plan and device. I concocted it for the salvation of the Church, and on principles so broad, that every honest man might dwell secure under its protective influence."[73]

The Illinois State Legislature approved the charter on December 16, 1840.[74] It contained several features that provided safety and power for Joseph Smith and his followers. The city council was composed of a mayor, four aldermen, and nine councilors.[75] This body had the authority to pass any laws that were "not repugnant to the Constitution of the United States" or to the state of Illinois.[76]

In addition, the municipal court was made up of the mayor and four aldermen.[77] This tribunal had the right to grant writs of habeas corpus, a power it sometimes exercised to free Joseph Smith when he was unjustly arrested by his enemies.[78] Section 25 of the charter granted the city council power to organize a militia named the Nauvoo Legion.[79] The *Times and Seasons* boasted that the Nauvoo Charter rendered "the most liberal provisions ever granted by a legislative assembly."[80]

Speaking of the charter, John C. Bennett reported that "every power we asked has been granted, every request gratified, every desire fulfilled."[81] One historian claimed, "The Saints relied on their Charter to be an unbreachable wall defending the rights of Zion."[82] Unfortunately, as time passed, "many of their non-Mormon neighbors came to view it as an offensive barrier."[83]

Joseph Smith's Involvement in Municipal Government

On February 1, 1841, the City of Nauvoo held its first municipal election. John C. Bennett had the distinction of being chosen the first mayor. He had been a member of the Church only a few months but was the one most responsible for steering the Nauvoo Charter through the legislature. A list of the other elected officials reads like a "Who's Who" in Latter-day Saint history. The four aldermen were William Marks, Samuel H. Smith, Daniel H. Wells, and Newel K. Whitney. The nine councilors were Joseph Smith, Hyrum Smith, Sidney Rigdon, Charles C. Rich, John T. Barnett, Wilson Law, Don Carlos Smith, John P. Greene, and Vinson Knight.[84] Some important Church leaders missing from this list were members of the Quorum of the Twelve Apostles. This is because most of them were on missions in the British Isles at the time.[85]

Joseph Smith served almost fifteen months on the city council before becoming mayor. During this time he was clearly the most energetic member of the body. For example, the council passed eleven ordinances during its first five meetings—all of them introduced by the Prophet.[86] At the first meeting of the city council held on Wednesday, February 3, 1841, Joseph Smith gave the opening prayer. New officers were then sworn in. After Mayor Bennett gave his lengthy inaugural address, the Prophet introduced bills to organize the Nauvoo Legion and the University of the City of Nauvoo. Both ordinances passed unanimously.

The Red Brick store is where the Nauvoo City Council held their meetings while Joseph Smith was mayor.

The council appointed Mayor Bennett as chancellor of the University with William Law as registrar. Joseph Smith, Sidney

Rigdon, Hyrum Smith, and twenty others were named regents. The Prophet then presented a resolution that formally thanked the governor and legislature for granting the Nauvoo Charter; it also thanked the citizens of Quincy for the kindness they showed the Saints during the Missouri persecutions.[87] The city council appointed Joseph Smith to serve as the chairman of several committees, including the one "on the Canal," "For Vacating the Town of Commerce," "Vending Spiritual Liquors," "Code of City Ordinances," and "Board of Health."[88]

Pursuant to the council's action, the Nauvoo Legion was organized the following day. On Thursday, February 4, 1841, at 10 A.M., a group of men gathered in Joseph Smith's office and unanimously elected him as lieutenant-general, or commander-in-chief of the militia. They also elected John C. Bennett major-general, Wilson Law brigadier-general of the first cohort, and Don Carlos Smith brigadier-general of the second cohort. After being sworn in, General Smith then appointed several lesser officers.[89]

Eleven days later, on February 15, at a meeting of the city council, the Prophet introduced "an ordinance in relation to temperance." During the meeting, he spoke at length on the use of liquors and showed that they were unnecessary and operated as a poison in the stomach."[90]

Later, on March 1, he sponsored another important bill titled "An Ordinance in Relation to Religious Societies." It read in part, "Be it ordained . . . that Catholics, Presbyterians, Methodists, Baptists, Latter-day Saints, Quakers, Episcopals, Universalists, Unitarians, Mohammedans, and all other religious sects and denominations whatever, shall have free toleration and equal privilege, in this city." Anyone guilty of "disturbing or interrupting any religious meeting within the limits of the city" could be fined up to $500 and imprisoned for six months.[91]

In July 1841, the members of the Quorum of the Twelve Apostles began returning to Nauvoo from their missions in Great Britain.[92] Soon thereafter, many of them became involved in the municipal government. On September 4, 1841, Brigham Young became a member of the city council, succeeding the Prophet's brother Don Carlos Smith, who died on August 7, at the age of twenty-five.[93]

On October 23, the city council added four additional councilors to its body, three of whom were members of the Quorum of the Twelve—John Taylor, Orson Pratt, and Heber C. Kimball. The fourth newcomer was a man named Hugh McFall.[94] On October 30, the council became even larger when it added three more Apostles to serve as councilors. They were Lyman Wight, Willard Richards, and Wilford Woodruff.

Brigham Young and the Quorum of the Twelve had the responsibility of organizing and overseeing the electioneer missionary force. Also, Brigham Young and most members of the Quorum of the Twelve personally campaigned for Joseph Smith.

During the same meeting, the council also elected two additional aldermen—Hiram Kimball and George W. Harris.[95] Thus, within eight days, the makeup of the city council changed significantly. The number of officers increased from fourteen members to twenty-three (a mayor, six alderman, and sixteen councilors), and all but three of the newly assigned officials were members of the Quorum of the Twelve.

A new phase in Joseph Smith's civic career began on January 22, 1842. On that date the council elected the Prophet vice mayor, whose duty it was to preside when the mayor was absent.[96] The Rules of Order of the City Council stated that the vice mayor should be elected by a "majority of the votes of the members present."[97] The minutes of the Nauvoo City Council show that the Prophet won by a vote of eighteen to three. Others receiving a vote were Hyrum Smith, Willard Richards, and Wilson Law.[98] The Prophet served in this office for four months before succeeding John C. Bennett as mayor.

The Prophet Becomes Mayor

The immediate circumstances leading to Joseph Smith becoming mayor were closely connected to the shameful fall of John C. Bennett. Few people had risen to prominence in Nauvoo as rapidly as did Bennett. During the week he was elected mayor, February 1, 1841, he was also appointed major-general of the Nauvoo Legion and chancellor of the University of Nauvoo.

Two months later, during general conference, he was sustained as an additional counselor to Joseph Smith in the First Presidency of the Church.[99] Unfortunately, he used his position for his own selfish and lustful desires. While serving as mayor, he seduced several married women into illicit sexual relations. He asserted that they could be his "spiritual" wives while still being married to their husbands, and he claimed that Joseph Smith sanctioned his behavior.[100]

Furthermore, on May 7, 1842, Bennett sought to put the Prophet in harm's way during a mock battle of the Nauvoo Legion.[101] Joseph Smith, however, recorded that "the gentle breathing of that Spirit, which whispered [to] me on parade" revealed the plot to have him assassinated and make Bennett the president of the Church.[102]

Soon thereafter the Nauvoo Stake High Council initiated an investigation into Bennett's behavior. It discovered that Bennett had used his position as a medical doctor to have improper, intimate contact with female patients. He also frequented houses of ill repute. One local newspaper even reported that he sought to poison the husband of a woman he hoped to pursue.[103]

In wake of these scandalous reports, Bennett decided to resign his position as mayor on May 17, 1842.[104] He appeared before Alderman Daniel H. Wells, who was a justice in Nauvoo, and wrote a sworn affidavit affirming that he never knew Joseph Smith "to countenance any improper conduct whatever, either in public or private." It also maintained that the Prophet never taught Bennett "that an illegal illicit intercourse with females was, under any circumstances, justifiable, and that [Bennett] never knew him so to teach others."[105]

Bennett's controversial resignation made it necessary to appoint a new mayor. A historical meeting of the Nauvoo City Council was held Thursday, May 19, 1842, for that purpose. News of Bennett's resignation had spread rapidly through the city, and the meeting was "filled with spectators" who had come with much anticipation.[106]

The first order of business was to formally accept Bennett's resignation, which was done unanimously. Then the council elected Joseph Smith as mayor by a vote of 18 to 1. William Marks received one vote.[107] Hyrum Smith was elected vice mayor, and William Smith was elected to the City Council in the place of his brother, Joseph. In addition, George A. Smith was elected as a councilor, replacing Hugh McFall, who had recently moved out of the city.[108]

In the midst of this memorable election, an unusual occurrence took place. Joseph Smith received and recorded a distressing revelation and gave it to Hiram Kimball, a member of the council. It contained the following warning: "Verily thus saith the Lord unto you my servant Joseph by the voice of my Spirit, Hiram Kimball has been insinuating evil. & forming evil opinions against you with others. & if he continue[s] in them he & they shall be accursed. for I am the Lord thy God & will stand by thee & bless thee. Amen."[109]

The Prophet's first order of business after being elected mayor was to speak "at some length concerning the evil reports which were abroad in the city concerning himself."[110] As a result, the council authorized him to establish a night watch for "counteracting the designs of [the] enemies."[111]

Next the new mayor called upon John C. Bennett to state if he had anything to say against Joseph Smith. Bennett replied that he "had no difficulty with the heads of the church." He added, "Any one who has said that I have stated that General Joseph Smith has given me authority to hold illicit intercourse with women is a Liar in the face of God."[112]

Before the meeting adjourned, Joseph Smith and the council extended appreciation to the former mayor: "Resolved . . . that this council tender a vote of thanks to General John C. Bennett, for his great zeal in having good and wholesome laws adopted for the government of this city, & for the faithful discharge of his duty while mayor of the same."[113] This seems to be a remarkable resolution in light of the fact that Bennett's deplorable behavior had caused the council so much distress.

Three days after being elected mayor, Joseph Smith read an article in the *Quincy Whig* announcing that Lilburn W. Boggs, former governor of Missouri, had been shot and critically wounded. Without any proof, the paper suggested that the Latter-day Saints were responsible: "One [rumor] . . . throws the crime upon the Mormons—from the fact, we suppose, that Mr. Boggs was governor at the time, and no small degree instrumental in driving them from the state." The article read, "Smith too, the Mormon prophet, as we understand, prophesied a year or so ago, [Boggs's] death by violent means. Hence there is plenty of foundation for rumor."[114]

Appalled by the article, Joseph Smith promptly went to the editor's office of the Nauvoo *Wasp* and submitted a forceful denial. He repudiated the accusation that he had prophesied the death of Lilburn Boggs by "violent means." The Prophet also declared that Boggs had not been shot by "my instrumentality," adding that "my hands are clean and my heart pure from the blood of all men."[115] This disclaimer was also published in the *Quincy Whig,* on June 4, 1842.[116]

Joseph anticipated that his enemies, living outside of Nauvoo and even beyond the boundaries of the state of Illinois, might come to his city, arrest him, and try to extradite him to another community or state to stand trial. Therefore, at a meeting held July 5, 1842, the city council passed a bill designed to protect the Prophet and other innocent members of the community. Titled "An Ordinance in Relation to Writs of Habeas Corpus," it emphasized a power originally granted to the city court by the Nauvoo Charter. It stipulated that "no citizen of this city shall be taken out of the city by writs without the privilege of investigation before the municipal court."

The bill forthrightly affirmed that it was issued to ensure that the people of Nauvoo "may in all cases have the right of trial in this city."[117] Joseph Smith, as mayor, readily signed the measure.

The Prophet's fear that his enemies would try to extradite him was realized during the last two years of his life. His opponents outside of Nauvoo tried to arrest him on several occasions. One of those adversaries was Lilburn Boggs, who surprisingly recovered from the attempted assassination. Soon thereafter, Boggs sought out a justice of the peace to issue an affidavit charging Orrin Porter Rockwell for the assault on his life.

In a second affidavit, Boggs accused Joseph Smith of being accessory before the fact."[118] Boggs then requested Missouri governor Thomas Reynolds "to make a demand on" Thomas Carlin, governor of Illinois, to deliver Joseph Smith and Rockwell to an authorized official of the state of Missouri.[119] Carlin agreed. On August 8, 1842, a deputy sheriff of neighboring Adams County went to Nauvoo and arrested the Prophet and Rockwell.

There was no attempt to resist arrest, but the Nauvoo Municipal Court issued a writ of habeas corpus, demanding that the deputy sheriff bring his prisoners before that tribunal. The deputy sheriff refused to obey the order, claiming Nauvoo City had no jurisdiction over him. He did, however, leave the prisoners with a Nauvoo City marshal and return to Adams County for additional orders from the governor. Joseph Smith and Orrin Porter Rockwell were allowed to go free, but the Prophet went into hiding for the next three months.[120]

In the meantime, other attempts were made to arrest the Prophet. Following one of these attempts, rumor spread that a sheriff from Missouri would come with a mob to apprehend Joseph. In response to this rumor, the Prophet, in his capacity as mayor, wrote to Wilson Law, the new major-general of the Nauvoo Legion, officially authorizing him to use force if necessary to "contest [the mob] at the point of the sword, with firm, undaunted and unyielding valor."[121]

During this time, friends of the Prophet tried to appeal his case to Governor Carlin, hoping that he might revoke the charges. Unfortunately, their plea fell on deaf ears. Instead, the unsympathetic governor offered a $200 bounty for Joseph Smith. In addition, Governor Reynolds, in Missouri, offered a $300 reward for the Prophet.[122] Soon thereafter, Thomas Ford replaced Carlin as governor of Illinois.

At this time Joseph Smith sought the counsel of Justin Butterfield, U.S. attorney for the district of Illinois, concerning the charges that had been brought against him by Boggs. In a formal, written response, Butterfield advised the Prophet to appeal to the new governor, believing that he might rescind the warrant for his arrest.[123] Governor Ford seemed sympathetic, but on advice of the court, he encouraged Joseph to appear before the district federal judge in Springfield. The governor also promised him protection if he would come.[124]

The Prophet complied with the request, and on December 26 voluntarily submitted to arrest at the hands of Wilson Law in Nauvoo.[125] He made the trip to Springfield with Law, Hyrum Smith, John Taylor, and others. Joseph then went before Judge Nathaniel Pope, who, on January 5, 1843, acquitted the Prophet and let him go free.[126]

Joseph Smith's legal problems and time in hiding only made his popularity soar among the Saints in Nauvoo. Upon his return to the city, the Quorum of the Twelve Apostles declared Tuesday, January 17, 1843, as a special "day of humiliation, fasting, praise, prayer and thanksgiving" for "the deliverance of [their] beloved president . . . from the oppression with which he [had] so long been bound." The Twelve directed the bishops of the various wards to bring their members together, hear reports from those who had been with the Prophet in Springfield, and take up collections to help pay for Joseph's legal fees.[127] These meetings were well attended, some to overflowing.[128]

Less than three weeks later, on Monday, February 6, 1843, Joseph Smith was elected mayor by unanimous vote. During the same election, the citizens chose Orson Spencer, Daniel H. Wells, George A. Smith, and Stephen Markham as aldermen. The nine men elected as councilors were Hyrum Smith, John Taylor, Orson Hyde, Orson Pratt, Sylvester Emmons, Heber C. Kimball, Benjamin Warrington, Daniel Spencer, and Brigham Young.[129] This municipal election was not only an indication of the tremendous popularity of Joseph Smith but also a reflection of the high esteem in which the Saints held the Twelve Apostles, six of whom were elected to office (Young, Kimball, Hyde, Pratt, Taylor, and George A. Smith).

Two weeks after his commanding victory in the mayor's race, Joseph seemed all the more determined to use political power for the good of his people, Speaking to a group of workmen on the Nauvoo Temple, the mayor declared, "It is our duty to concentrate all our influence to make popular that which is sound and good. . . . 'Tis right, politically, for a man who has influence to use it. . . . From henceforth I will maintain all the influence I can get. In relation to politics I will speak as a man; but in relation to religion I will speak in authority."[130]

B. H. Roberts claimed that immediately following this election "Nauvoo was rapidly approaching the high watermark of her prosperity."[131] But unfortunately, troubled times were on the horizon. In an attempt to retrieve the power it had originally granted to the city, the Illinois House of Representatives tried to revoke the Nauvoo Charter. On March 3, 1843, it voted 58 to 33 in favor of the action.[132] On the following day, fortunately, the Senate voted by the narrow margin of seventeen to sixteen to retain the charter.[133]

Later that year some Missourians kidnapped two citizens of Hancock County, and rumors began to circulate that they planned to invade Nauvoo and kidnap even more. On December 8, 1843, Willard Richards and Phillip B. Lewis appeared before Mayor Joseph Smith and afterward issued an affidavit, confirming that the rumors were true. The mayor immediately began to prepare for what one historian termed a possible "border war."[134]

Joseph issued a written notification to Henry G. Sherwood, the city marshal, authorizing him to use part of the Nauvoo Legion to protect the city. Sherwood was willing to carry out the request but was worried about protocol. He wrote back to the mayor, asking him to order Wilson Law, major-general of the Nauvoo Legion, to ready the troops and make them available to the city marshal. Joseph followed through, and the legion was put on alert.[135]

The mayor then met with the city council. Anticipating that Joseph Smith was the prime candidate to be kidnapped, the council, under his direction, passed "an extra ordinance for the extra case of Joseph Smith and others." It asserted that "if any person or persons shall come with process . . . founded upon the . . . Missouri difficulties, to arrest . . . Joseph Smith, he or they so offending shall be subject to . . . [arrest] by any officer of the city, with or without process, and tried by the Municipal Court . . . and if found guilty, sentenced to imprisonment in the city prison for life." The bill also provided that the convicts could "only be pardoned by the Governor, with the consent of the Mayor of said city."[136]

City officials kept Governor Ford informed of the Missourians' threats to invade Nauvoo, but it soon became obvious that Ford was not their friend and that they could not depend on the state to help protect their city. Under the direction of the mayor and the city council, a unique but radical plan was introduced for the security of Nauvoo.

On December 21, 1843, city officials drew up an ordinance petitioning the U.S. Congress to make Nauvoo a federal municipal territory of the United States—essentially an independent city-state under the protection of the U.S. government. The Nauvoo Legion would also become an official unit of the federal army, but under the direction of the mayor. The ordinance declared, "All rights[,] powers[,] privileges and immunities belonging to Territories, and not repugnant to the Constitution of the United States, are hereby granted and secured to the inhabitants of the city of Nauvoo. . . . That the mayor of Nauvoo be . . . empowered by . . . the President of the United States . . .

to call to his aid a sufficient number of United States forces, in connection with the Nauvoo Legion, to repel the invasion of mobs, keep the public peace, and protect the innocent."[137] The council then authorized Orson Pratt to present the petition to the U.S. Congress.[138] Not surprisingly, the petition was never acted upon.

In another attempt to build up security for Nauvoo, the mayor and city council increased the police force with an additional forty men, the "high policeman" (chief of police) being Jonathan Dunham. They were sworn "to support the Constitution of the United States and the State of Illinois, and obey . . . the instructions of the Mayor."[139] Joseph Smith spoke to them at length, warning them not only of enemies in Missouri but also of traitors within the city. He had an interesting philosophy for preventing corruption within law enforcement. He explained, "If any one offered a bribe to a policeman, the city will pay that policeman twice the amount offered for the information, when reported to the Mayor."[140]

In late 1843, Joseph Smith's political thinking began to expand beyond his duties as mayor of Nauvoo. During this time he became increasingly interested in the upcoming presidential election. Indeed, early in 1844 he would decide to run for president himself. Therefore, during the last five months of his life he not only served as mayor of Nauvoo but also ran for president of the United States.

The Road to Becoming a Candidate for President

In anticipation of the 1844 presidential election, *The Times and Seasons* published an editorial on October 1, 1843, titled "Who Shall Be Our Next President?" It did not suggest any specific names but concluded that the candidate must be a "man who will be most likely to render us assistance in obtaining redress for our grievances."[141]

On November 4, 1843, Joseph Smith wrote letters to John C. Calhoun, Lewis Cass, Richard M. Johnson, Henry Clay, and Martin Van Buren, the five leading candidates for the presidency of the United States. Each letter talked of the persecutions the Latter-day Saints had suffered at the hands of the state of Missouri and then asked a pointed question: *"What will be your rule of action relative to us as a people,"* should fortune favor your ascension to the chief magistracy?"[142]

General Joseph Smith for U.S. President Buttons

The letters said essentially the same thing, with one exception. To Martin Van Buren, the Prophet could not resist adding a postscript, in which he wanted to know "whether your views or feeling have changed since the subject matter of this communication was presented you in your then official capacity at Washington, in the year 1841 [1839–40] and by you treated with coldness, indifference, and neglect, bordering on contempt."[143]

Van Buren and Johnson never responded to Joseph Smith's letters, but Calhoun, Cass, and Clay did. Yet those who replied were not willing to pledge their support to the Church. The correspondence between Joseph Smith and John C. Calhoun is of particular interest because it brings into focus their contrasting views on the powers of the national government—something that would become a vital issue during the Prophet's campaign for president.

Calhoun wrote, "The case [of the Mormon persecution in Missouri] does not come within the jurisdiction of the Federal Government, which is one of *limited and specific powers.*"[144] To this, Joseph Smith responded with a much different interpretation: "Congress has power to protect the nation against foreign invasion and *internal broil . . . and the President has as much power . . . as Washington had to march against the 'whiskey boys at Pittsburgh,' or General Jackson had to send an armed force to suppress the rebellion of South Carolina.*"[145] Calhoun made no further reply.

When he determined that none of the leading candidates for president would pledge his support in gaining redress for the Saints, the Prophet held a historic meeting in the mayor's office on January 29, 1844. During that meeting, which was attended by the Quorum of the Twelve Apostles and other leaders, Willard Richards made a motion that Joseph Smith should run for the presidency on an independent electoral ticket and that those present should use "all honorable means in [their] power to secure his election."[146] Thus formally began one of the most intriguing third-party campaigns for president of the United States in the history of the nation.

The Platform

Joseph wasted little time in preparing a platform for his campaign. On the same day he formally decided to run for president, he met with William W. Phelps and dictated to him the headings for a pamphlet titled *General Smith's Views of the Powers and Policy of the Government of the United States*.[147] This pamphlet became the foundation document for the Prophet's presidential platform.

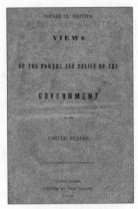

A pamphlet distributed by Joseph Smith.

Many have written about William W. Phelps's involvement in writing *General Smith's Views*. One scholar maintains that "Joseph Smith relied heavily upon" Phelps in writing *Views* and other political documents.[148] Phelps had a superficial knowledge of foreign phrases that he loved to insert in many of the documents he wrote. *Views* is full of such phrases, which B. H. Roberts attributes to Phelps.[149] These literary antics annoyed Roberts, who often edited them out in his *History of the Church*. On one occasion, Roberts wrote that Phelps "had some smattering knowledge of languages, which he was ever fond of displaying. . . . [However, these injected phrases were] in no way germane to the subjects of which they treat, and are not really the work of President Smith."[150]

So how much of *General Smith's Views* did Joseph Smith actually write? This same question could be asked about the greater part of all the writings attributed to the Prophet. Dean Jessee explains that "the Mormon leader depended upon clerks to do most of his writing"; hence, "the variety in the Smith papers, fluctuating between holograph, dictated, and ghostwritten prose creates a challenge for those who . . . face issues of actual authorship."[151]

Joseph Smith made few statements about how *Views* was written. On January 29, 1844, he said, "I dictated to Brother Phelps the heads of my pamphlet, entitled, 'Views on the Powers and Policy of the Government of the United States.'"[152] Then, nine days later, on February 7, he wrote, "I completed and signed my 'Views.'"[153] How much Joseph Smith or William Phelps actually wrote can only be guessed.

It is correct to assume that Phelps did most of the actual writing. However, Joseph Smith gave considerable guidance and input to the project, espoused the basic concepts of the platform, and assumed ultimate responsibility for the ideas in the document. The Prophet dictated the headings of the pamphlet to Phelps, and almost every time Joseph refers to the document, he calls it "My 'Views'" or "My Pamphlet." For example, on February 5, 1844, he wrote: "Called at my office in the evening and revised *My 'Views.'*"[154]

The fact that Joseph signed the document also signifies that he accepted responsibility for its contents. As we analyze the pamphlet, therefore, it seems that we are bound to assume that the basic concepts of the platform either originated with Joseph or, at the very least, were espoused by him. On the other hand, much (if not most) of the actual writing and a great deal of the phraseology can probably be attributed to William Phelps.

General Smith's Views of the Powers and Policy of the Government of the United States is strictly a political document. Joseph Smith made no mention of his religious teachings in the pamphlet. The use of the title "General" (of the Nauvoo Legion) rather than "Prophet" or "President" set the tone for the tract. The pamphlet said nothing about Joseph Smith's spiritual experiences and did not mention The Church of Jesus Christ of Latter-day Saints. In fact, just a few months before the booklet was published, Joseph declared, "The Lord has not given me a revelation concerning politics. I have not asked him for one."[155]

Views was, essentially, an attempt to give pragmatic solutions to many of the nation's most pressing problems. Joseph advocated giving power to the president to suppress mobs. He also favored abolishing slavery, reducing both the number and pay of the House of Representatives, reforming the prison system, eliminating courts-martial for desertion, forming a national bank, and annexing Oregon and Texas.

The most important plank in his platform concerned the powers of the president of the United States. Surprisingly, some who have written about that platform did not consider this issue at all,[156] while others assert that "the major plank of the Prophet's platform was the elimination of slavery."[157]

However, when the Prophet met with President Van Buren in 1840, he was not angered by Van Buren's position on slavery but rather by his refusal to exercise presidential powers to help the Saints. Similarly, in November 1843, when the Prophet wrote to the five leading presidential candidates, the only question he asked them was, "What will be your rule of action relative to us as a people" if you are elected?[158] These five letters asked nothing about their position on slavery. Furthermore, Joseph Smith attacked Senator Calhoun for his conservative views on the "limited and specific powers" of the federal government.[159] Again we should note that the Prophet said nothing about Calhoun's views on slavery.

Joseph Smith put this matter of presidential powers in perspective on the evening of February 8, 1844, the first night his *Views* were publicly read. The Prophet addressed the meeting as follows:

"I would not have suffered my name to have been used by my friends on anywise as President of the United States, or candidate for that office, if I and my friends could have had the privilege of enjoying our religious and civil rights as American citizens, even those rights which the Constitution guarantees unto all her citizens alike. But this as a people we have been denied from the beginning. Persecution has rolled upon our heads from time to time, from portions of the Untied States, like peals of thunder, because of our religion; and *no portion of this government as yet has stepped forward for our relief. And in view of these things, I feel it to be my right and privilege to obtain what influence and power I can, lawfully, in the United States, for the protection of injured innocence.*[160]

Notice that the only motivation the Prophet cited for running was to gain power to protect his injured people. He said nothing about slavery or any other issue.

Specifically, *General Smith's Views* proposed to give "the president full powers to send an army to suppress mobs; and the states the authority to repeal and impugn the relic of folly, which makes it necessary for the governor of a state to make the demand of the President for troops, in case of invasion or rebellion."[161] Here the Prophet was referring to Article IV, Section 4, of the U.S. Constitution, which states that the federal government shall protect the states against "domestic violence" only on application of the state legislature or governor. Speaking of this article, Joseph Smith observed, "The governor himself may be a mobber and, instead of being punished, as he should be for murder and treason, he may destroy the very lives, riches and property he should protect."[162]

The Prophet felt so strongly about this matter that on one occasion he even advocated capital punishment for public officials who declined to protect the lives and property of citizens: "The Constitution should contain a provision that every officer of the government who should neglect or refuse to extend the protection guaranteed in the Constitution should be subject to capital punishment; and then the president of the United States would not say, '*Your cause is just, but I can do nothing for you*' [or] a governor issue exterminating orders."[163]

Slavery, though not the primary focus, was another important issue in Joseph Smith's platform. The Prophet recommended the abolition of slavery by the year 1850, at the latest. He would have Congress "pay every man a reasonable price for his slaves out of the surplus revenue arising from the sale of public lands, and from the deduction of pay from members of Congress. Break off the shackles from the poor black man, and hire them to labor like other human beings."[164]

Some might criticize this proposal as being economically impractical. Such critics should be reminded that the way the United States ultimately settled the slavery issue was through civil war—a conflict that cost more than fifteen billion dollars and more than 600,000 lives.[165] It was the most devastating war in American history, a conflict that left the South in economic ruin and implanted bitterness and hatred in the hearts of millions. As historian David Potter once said, "Slavery was dead, secession was dead, and six hundred thousand men were dead."[166] In retrospect, it would seem that Joseph Smith's solution to the slavery issue was certainly more sensible than the Civil War.

According to *General Smith's Views*, the slavery problem and the issue of congressional reform were closely related. The Prophet wanted to raise money to purchase slaves from their owners, in part by reducing the number of congressmen and their pay. Joseph advocated keeping two senators from each state but having only two representatives for every one million people.[167] In 1844, there were 223 representatives and 52 senators representing 26 states. The population of the United States was approximately 20 million. The Prophet's proposal would have reduced the House of Representatives from 223 to 40.[168] He believed a legislative body this size would "do more business than the army that now occupy the halls of the national Legislature."[169]

Joseph Smith also suggested that the pay for congress-men be reduced to two dollars a day (except Sundays). "That is more than a farmer gets, and he lives honestly."[170] The pay for members of Congress in 1844 was eight dollars a day.[171] The Prophet's suggested reduction in congressional member-ship and pay would have generated $553,384 for buying slaves. The proposal would seem to imply that Joseph believed that the issues of emancipation, as well as efficiency and economy in government, were more important than having large numbers of local representatives in Congress.

Views also recommended reform for the nation's prison sys-tem: "Let penitentiaries be turned into seminaries of learning," the Prophet declared. "Rigor and seclusion never do as much to reform the propensities of men as [would] reason and friend-ship."[172] Joseph believed that those who had broken the law should be put to work on "roads, public works, or any place where the culprit [could] be taught more wisdom and more virtue; and become more enlightened."[173] He also wanted to do away with imprisonment for debt, which was a lingering problem in some states.[174] The Prophet's progressive position on prison reform reflected not only his desire to improve society in general but also his compassion for those who had broken the law.

Military reform was another plank. The Prophet wanted to abolish the practice in the army and navy of trying men by court-martial for desertion: "If a soldier or marine runs away, send him his wages, with this instruction, that his country will never trust him again, he has forfeited his honor. Make honor the standard with all men." Joseph continued, "Be sure that good is rendered for evil in all cases: and the whole nation . . . will rise up with righteousness: and be respected as wise and worthy on earth."[175] Granted, this recommendation was un-commonly idealistic, but what a wonderful world it would be if everybody endeavored to "be sure that good is rendered for evil in all cases."

The concept of a national bank was a plank that the Prophet seemed to be particularly pleased with. On the evening of Monday, February 5, 1844, two days before *General Smith's Views* was completed, the Prophet wrote, "I was the first one who publicly proposed a national bank on the principles set forth in [the] pamphlet."[176]

He recommended, first, that a national bank be established "with branches in each state and territory"; second, that the officers "be elected yearly" and paid "two dollars per day for services"; third, that the several banks not be permitted to "issue any more bills than the amount of capital stock in [their] vaults"; fourth, that "the net gain of the Central bank shall be applied to the national revenue, and that of the branches to the states and territories' revenues"; and fifth, "that the bills shall be par throughout the nation," which he believed would cure the problem of "brokerage."[177]

The Prophet's feelings about a strong national banking system, no doubt, stemmed from his experience with the Kirtland Safety Society in 1837—an attempt to establish a banking institution that failed miserably and disillusioned numerous members of the Church.[178] Joseph hoped to prevent such misfortune in the future.

The final plank of his platform dealt with foreign affairs. Joseph Smith was an expansionist who believed in the immediate annexation of the Oregon Territory: "Oregon belongs to the government honorably; and when we have the red man's consent, let the Union spread from east to the west sea."[179]

His position on Texas, however, was somewhat different. He advocated annexing the Lone Star State only if it first petitioned Congress to be admitted. He even extended the same invitation to Canada and Mexico, but only on petition.[180] The

Prophet's motivation seemed to be a desire to bring these political entities under the influence of the U.S. Constitution, which, he taught, was an inspired document (see D&C 101:77, 80).

General Smith's Views is an intriguing document. With the luxury of hindsight, we can see that many of his proposals came to pass, although not necessarily in the way he had hoped. The power of the presidency was increased by Abraham Lincoln during the Civil War; that same bloody conflict also emancipated the slaves. The penal system has improved, although not to the extent that Joseph prescribed. And, of course, Oregon and Texas soon became part of the Union.

Elder John A. Widtsoe's evaluation of *Views* seems appropriate: "This campaign document is an intelligent, comprehensive, forward-looking statement of policies, worthy of a trained statesman. Many of the Prophet's recommendations have been adopted in the progressive passage of the years. All of them are reasonable and sound."[181]

On the evening of February 8, 1844, William Phelps read *General Smith's Views* publicly for the first time. Joseph Smith, Orson Hyde, and John Taylor then spoke, after which all in attendance at the gathering voted unanimously to support the Prophet's platform.[182] By February 24, Joseph had 1,500 copies of the pamphlet printed,[183] and three days later he had copies mailed to the president of the United States and his cabinet, the justices of the Supreme Court, "senators, representatives, principal newspapers in the United States, . . . and many postmasters."[184] During the next four months, at least forty-five newspapers located in twenty-two states in the Union published articles concerning Joseph Smith's *Views*.[185] Obviously, the newspapers printed mixed responses, but many were favorable.[186]

On March 11, 1844, Joseph Smith called a special meeting in the lodge room over Henry Miller's house. Twenty-three people attended, including Hyrum Smith and seven members of the Quorum of the Twelve.[187] During this meeting the Prophet organized a "special council" that soon became known as the Council of Fifty because of the number of people who were members.

According to one history, "At least as early as 1842 those closest to Joseph Smith anticipated the establishment of a political entity outside the regular organization of the Church, although dominated by priesthood leaders. Known as the Kingdom of God, it would prepare politically for the coming of the Savior and the Millennium." The history explains, "The Council of Fifty, after its organization in early 1844, was the governing body of this political 'kingdom.' Though critics of the Church misinterpreted the actions of the council, its main concern was to influence the establishment of righteous government that would protect the rights of all, including the Saints, and prepare for the Millennium."[188]

Soon all the members of the Quorum of the Twelve became members of the organization.[189] The Council of Fifty was given "some practical responsibilities for organizing Joseph Smith's presidential campaign."[190] However, because all of the Apostles were members of both the Quorum of the Twelve and the Council of Fifty, "the distinction between the political and ecclesiastical kingdoms blurred."[191] Nevertheless, the Apostles and others enthusiastically moved forward with plans for the campaign.[192]

The Campaign Strategy

When the decision was made to have Joseph Smith run for president of the United States, the Prophet responded with the following instructions: "If you attempt to accomplish this, you must send every man in the city who is able to speak in public throughout the land to electioneer and make stump speeches, advocate the 'Mormon' religion, purity of elections, and call upon the people to stand by the law and put down mobocracy." He further directed: "After the April Conference we will have General Conferences all over the nation. . . . Hyrum, Brigham, Parley and Taylor must go. . . . There is oratory enough in the Church to carry me into the presidential chair first slide."[193]

With this declaration, the Prophet immediately established the unique role of those who would participate in his campaign. They would not only "electioneer and make stump speeches" but would also "advocate the 'Mormon' religion." In other words, those who would campaign for Joseph Smith would also be involved in preaching the gospel. In addition, members of the Quorum of the Twelve would be involved in the endeavor. Finally, many of the campaign activities would be organized in conjunction with regional "general conferences."

This concept of interweaving spiritual sermons with presidential politics carried on into the next general conference in Nauvoo. In that assembly on April 9, 1844, Hyrum Smith admonished the Saints to build their temple, as well as to lift up their "voices like thunder" and use their "power and influence" to elect Joseph Smith president.[194] Brigham Young likewise emphasized construction of the temple but then said that the Church was going to send elders "to preach the Gospel and electioneer" for Joseph Smith.[195] Heber C. Kimball then stood and spoke of the importance of preaching the first principles of the gospel. However, he concluded by saying, "We are going to arrange a plan for Conferences, and we design to send Elders to all the different States to get up meetings and protracted meetings, and electioneer for Joseph to be the next President."[196]

Near the end of the meeting, when Church leaders called for volunteers to serve political/religious missions, 244 people stepped forward.[197] Thus began something unique in American as well as Mormon history—missionaries called to campaign for their presidential candidate and, at the same time, proselytize for their church.

During the next few days, additional missionaries were called, bringing the grand total to at least 337.[198] Surprisingly, little has been written about the relative size and strength of this missionary force. These 337 electioneer missionaries, added to the number of those who had been called to serve traditional missions during the same year, brought the total number of missionaries to 586 in 1844.[199] This was, by far, the largest number of missionaries called to serve in a single year up to that time.

To put this number into perspective, the average number of missionaries set apart in a single year prior to 1843 was sixty-one. The fewest number of missionaries set apart in a single year during the same period was sixteen (in 1830 and 1838). The highest number of missionaries set apart in any single year prior to 1843 was 111, in 1834. Looking ahead after 1844, it would be more than fifty years before the Church would call more than 586 missionaries in the same year (746 were called in

1895).[200] Missionary statistics in the early years of the Church were not nearly as accurate as they are today, but the numbers for 1844 are nevertheless quite impressive. Not only the number but also the quality of the missionaries called was striking. All the members of the Quorum of the Twelve, except John Taylor and Willard Richards, served as electioneer missionaries. Brigham Young, Heber C. Kimball, Orson Hyde, Parley P. Pratt, William Smith, Orson Pratt, John E. Page, Wilford Woodruff, George A. Smith, and Lyman Wight were some of the greatest missionaries in the history of the Church.

On April 15 these electioneer missionaries were assigned to all twenty-six states in the Union and the Wisconsin Territory. The state of New York was assigned the most missionaries (forty-seven), while the Wisconsin Territory received the fewest (one).[201] The Apostles also designated one or two elders to preside over the missionaries of each state.[202] The Quorum of the Twelve scheduled a series of forty-seven conferences to be held in fifteen different states and the nation's capital, starting in Quincy, Illinois, on May 4, and ending in Washington, D.C., on September 15.[203] The elders who presided over the various states were to organize the conferences.[204]

Originally the Twelve Apostles did not assign themselves to specific conferences but stated that they would "devote the season to traveling, and [would] attend as many conferences as possible."[205] They were to "present before the people" the Prophet's published platform and were to "be faithful in preaching the gospel in its simplicity and beauty."[206] As it turned out, the elders would usually preach the gospel during the conferences and then schedule political rallies either the day before or the day after the general conferences in the various regions.

Even before the Apostles and many others departed on electioneer missions, enthusiasm for Joseph Smith's campaign began to accelerate, especially in an around Nauvoo. One of the popular indicators took place on the riverboats of the Mississippi River. Often their passengers would participate in unofficial straw polls or mock voting, perhaps the closest thing they had to the Gallup Polls of today. The Prophet recorded the findings of several of these straw polls in his history. The following, published in the *Nauvoo Neighbor*, is perhaps the most interesting:

> "General Joseph Smith, the acknowledged modern Prophet, has got them all in the rear; and from the common mode of testing the success of candidates for the Presidency, to wit., by steamboat elections, he (Smith) will beat all the other aspirants to that office two to one. We learn from the polls of the steamboat *Osprey*, on her last trip to this city, that the vote stood for General Joseph Smith, 20 gents and 5 ladies; Henry Clay, 16 gents and 4 ladies; Van Buren, 7 gents and 0 ladies."[207]

The next important official event of Joseph Smith's campaign was the state convention held May 17, 1844, in Nauvoo. Delegates representing all twenty-six states and ten Illinois counties attended. Most delegates, however, were citizens of Nauvoo, representing states they had previously lived in. During that convention, Joseph Smith was formally nominated as president, and Sidney Rigdon was nominated as vice president.

The delegates made plans to have a national convention in Baltimore, Maryland, on July 13 and appointed Willard Richards, John M. Bernhisel, William W. Phelps, and Lucian R. Foster to serve as a central committee of correspondence for the campaign. The featured speaker was John S. Reid, a non-Mormon lawyer who had defended the Prophet in his first prosecution in the state of New York.[208] This convention seemed to energize those in attendance, and soon literally hundreds of political missionaries were campaigning for Joseph Smith throughout the United States.

Electioneer Missionaries: The Quorum of the Twelve Campaigns for the Prophet

The Quorum of the Twelve had the responsibility of organizing and overseeing the great political missionary force that campaigned for Joseph Smith. Most of the Apostles themselves electioneered vigorously on behalf of their prophet.

Traveling to the Eastern States

During the spring of 1844 the Apostles began their missions to the East. They did not leave all together but rather commenced their journeys at different times, taking diverse routes. Wilford Woodruff and George A. Smith were the first two Apostles to depart. On May 9, Elder Woodruff recorded: "It has been my lot to travel in the vineyard [every] summer with one exception for the last ten years of my [life]."[209]

He parted from his family, accompanied by George A. Smith, Jedediah M. Grant, Ezra Thayer, and Thayer's son. Elder Woodruff added to his journal more than two months later: "I this day took the last Parting hand & look with the Prophet and Patriarch at their own dwelling. [Oh] what a look Joseph gave me. Ah he knew what I did not."[210] That was the last time Elder Woodruff saw Joseph and Hyrum before they were martyred.

Elders Woodruff and Smith began making their way east across Illinois, preaching the gospel as they went at such places as La Harpe and Toulon. Their first political rally was held in a courthouse at Ottowa, Illinois, on May 17. George A. Smith lectured on *General Smith's Views* to an audience of about 300 and was apparently well received. Evidently, Wilford Woodruff continued on to LaSalle, where he preached the gospel to a branch of about fifty members from Norway.[211]

On May 18 and 19, they held their first conference in Newark, Kendall County, Illinois. This would be the first of four conferences they would hold on their trip east before Wilford Woodruff would arrive in Boston at the end of June. The pattern they followed at this conference would be repeated many times by most of the Apostles as they traveled through the country. First they held a traditional Church conference, which was on Saturday and Sunday. Here they took care of ecclesiastical business and preached the gospel.

In Newark, 133 members from eight different branches attended. The Apostles ordained eight elders, one priest, and two teachers. Wilford Woodruff "instructed the elders to be careful to preach the first principle[s] of the gospel and the doctrin[e] of Christ & not spend their time in warring with the opinions of other men."[212]

Then, the day following the ecclesiastical conference, they held a political gathering in a schoolhouse at Newark. Henry Jacobs read Joseph's *Views,* and David Fulmer, Wilford Woodruff, and George A. Smith addressed the audience. When they had finished, a "Dr. Smith arose and [harangued] the people in a vile manner & raised a row. There was some prospect of fighting, but with soft words [they] turned away wrath & returned home in peace."[213]

On May 21, the brethren rode to Joliet, Illinois, where they spoke at a political rally held in a large schoolroom. George A. Smith conducted the meeting and introduced Wilford Woodruff.[214] "I arose & felt inspired by the spirit of God," wrote Elder Woodruff. He spoke on a variety of political topics, in-

cluding the Mormon persecutions and *General Smith's Views.*
The concluding speakers were David Fulmer and George A.
Smith. They "had the best attention of the people & a good
impression was made."[215]

By May 28, they arrived in Kalamazoo, Michigan, the
"finest town" they had seen since they left Nauvoo. The "improvements [were] after the eastern fashion."[216] From there they
went to the small village of Comstoc, where they stayed for the
next five days, mostly at the home of Ezekiel Lee, the presiding
elder in the area. During that time, members and missionaries in the region began to gather for a conference. On May 31,
they held a political meeting in Brother Lee's barn. Charles C.
Rich conducted and Henry Jacobs read Joseph's *Views.* Wilford
Woodruff "spoke of the foundation laid by [Joseph] Smith to
unite the nation." He was followed by George A. Smith and
David Fulmer. They felt that they had "left a good impression
upon the minds of the people."[217]

The next two days they held a Church conference that was
attended by 126 members from nine branches. They sustained
Charles C. Rich and Harvey Green to preside over the state of
Michigan. In the first session alone at least eleven people spoke,
and the elders were strictly charged "to keep within the limits
of the first principles of the gospel & let mysteries alone."[218]

After the last session, on Sunday, June 2, Elder Woodruff
wrote that they "had an interesting conference and a good time
with the Saints." He was also impressed that Charles C. Rich
had "manifested much wisdom in [concocting] his plans in
carrying out his work both on politics & religion, in the State
of Michigan." The elders then "took up a collection" to assist
them on their mission and obtained $4.50.[219]

For the next five days they traveled across the state toward
Pleasant Valley, Michigan, where they would hold their third
conference. Along the way they stayed with members of the

Church, ordained an eighty-seven-year-old man to be a high priest, and administered to a sick child. During this part of the journey they did not preach the gospel or hold any political rallies.[220] Then, on June 8 and 9, they held their conference in Pleasant Valley. Eighty-nine members from six branches attended. The following day they had a political meeting, but no details were recorded other than that they "had a good time."[221]

A week later, on June 15 and 16, Elders Woodruff and Smith held their fourth conference, this time in Franklin, Michigan. A total of 170 members from 12 branches attended, but there is no record of the traveling Apostles holding a political rally either before or after the conference. On June 17 Elder Woodruff wrote a letter to his wife, Phebe, and sent it in a package with twelve silver dollars. He gave the package to Elder Smith, who parted company with Elder Woodruff and returned to Nauvoo before campaigning further.[222] Wilford continued traveling east by way of Cleveland, Buffalo, Rochester, and Albany before arriving in Boston on June 26, 1844.[223]

During much of the time that Wilford Woodruff and George A. Smith had been traveling through Illinois and Michigan, four other Apostles—Brigham Young, Heber C. Kimball, Lyman Wight, and William Smith—had also been journeying to the East by way of such places as St. Louis, Cincinnati, and Pittsburgh. Three of those Apostles (Young, Kimball, and Wight) had left Nauvoo on May 21, 1844, "amidst the acclamations of three cheers from the shore, 'Joseph Smith, the next president of the United States.'"[224]

They headed down the Mississippi River toward St. Louis on a steamer named *Osprey*, which had about 165 passengers. The first day on the boat, Lyman Wight delivered "a political address" that established the "right Joseph Smith had to the presidential chair."[225] Elder Wight claimed that his speech met with "the entire satisfaction of nearly all the passengers on board."[226] During his talk he was "frequently interrupted with loud laughing and clapping hands, by way of approbation."[227]

A political straw poll taken on the *Osprey* after Lyman Wight spoke showed that "Joseph Smith received a large majority over all other candidates."[228] However, since the steamer was coming from Nauvoo, it is fair to assume that a significant number of those aboard were members of the Church.

The next day, May 22, the elders arrived at St. Louis. Here Brigham Young and Heber C. Kimball met with a large branch of the Church that had almost seven hundred members. They did not record details of the meeting except to say they "instructed them spiritually and politically."[229]

While in St. Louis, they were joined by another Apostle, William Smith. On May 23, Elders Young, Kimball, Wight, and Smith boarded another boat, the *Louis Phillippe*, headed for Cincinnati. "There were at first some little prejudices" against them until Brigham Young spoke on the principles of the gospel, which evidently alleviated the animosity.[230]

While they were on the steamboat, Lyman Wight struck up a conversation with David Guard, an affluent businessman from Lawrenceburgh, Indiana. Elder Wight found that Guard had been one of the earliest settlers in Cincinnati and was worth between two and three hundred thousand dollars. Lyman gave the man two copies of *General Smith's Views*, which greatly impressed him. The gentleman promised to have *Views* published in both Lawrenceburgh papers, which were housed in buildings that he owned. "If they did not" publish it, Guard maintained, the editors "would have to seek shelter elsewhere."[231]

The steamer arrived in Cincinnati on May 26, and that evening Elders Young and Kimball went on shore to meet with members of the Church, while Elder Wight stayed behind to transfer their luggage to the *Neptune*, a boat soon bound for

Pittsburgh.[232] The next day Elders Young, Kimball, and Wight held a Church conference in Cincinnati at 8 A.M. All three of them spoke "on the subject of politics and perseverance in duty, and the great necessity of reform in government."[233] They also instructed local elders to print two thousand copies of Joseph's *Views* and charged them to distribute the pamphlets "with the velocity of lightning and the voice of thunder."[234]

By 10 A.M. that same day, the Apostles were on a steamboat heading for Pittsburgh. While on board, Lyman Wight gave an address on the Book of Mormon "and the present situation of the world." On that voyage another mock vote was taken for president of the United States, and according to Wight, "a large majority of the votes were given" to Joseph Smith.[235]

The four Apostles reached Pittsburgh on May 30, 1844. The next day Brigham Young parted company with the other three. Heber C. Kimball, William Smith, and Lyman Wight went on to Washington, D.C. They traveled by "steamer, stage and railway," wrote Lyman, "preaching . . . and thorning everybody with politics that came in our way."[236] These three would reunite with Brigham Young in Boston four weeks later. Meanwhile, on June 1 and 2, Elder Young attended a Church conference in Pittsburgh with another Apostle, John E. Page.[237]

After those meetings, Elder Young turned west for a time and spent the next week in Ohio. In Shalorsville he stayed with the Salmon Gee family and spoke to the townspeople about Joseph's *Views*.[238] The next day, June 7, lawyers and doctors called on him to obtain copies of the pamphlet. That same day he met with Lorenzo Snow in Mantua and preached in Hiram, a former center of Latter-day Saint activity, where Joseph Smith and Sidney Rigdon had been tarred and feathered in 1832.[239] For the next few days he visited with family and even preached in the Kirtland Temple. He then proceeded to New England by way of Buffalo, Albany, and New York City, arriving in Boston on Sunday, June 16, 1844.[240]

While Brigham Young and many of the Apostles had been making their way east across the United States, persecution against the Church was mounting in Nauvoo. In the early part of 1844, some of Joseph Smith's closest associates had apostatized from the Church, including William Law, second counselor in the First Presidency. On June 7, 1844, Law and several cohorts published the *Nauvoo Expositor* in an effort to defame Joseph Smith and promote their own causes.[241]

Among other things, they charged the Prophet with abusing political and ecclesiastical power, teaching plural marriage and plurality of gods, violating the separation of church and state, establishing a secret society for religious purposes, organizing an inquisition, teaching spiritual wifery, and having a hostile spirit toward Missouri.[242] On June 10, the Nauvoo City Council authorized Joseph Smith, in his capacity as mayor, to have the *Nauvoo Expositor* "removed without delay."[243] Joseph immediately ordered the city marshal to destroy the press of the infamous periodical, which was done within two hours.[244]

Joseph Smith, as mayor of Nauvoo, ordered the city marshal to destroy the press of the Nauvoo Expositor. This led to Joseph Smith's arrest and martyrdom.

In response, the *Warsaw Signal*, an anti-Mormon newspaper, proclaimed: "War and extermination is inevitable! Citizens arise, one and all!!! . . . We have no time for comment: every man will make his own. *Let it be made with powder and ball!!!*"[245] On June 18, in this charged atmosphere, Joseph put the city under martial law.[246] Two days later the Prophet wrote letters to all the Apostles serving missions in the east, asking them "to come home immediately."[247] However, before any of the letters could reach the Apostles, Joseph Smith was murdered in Carthage Jail.

In Boston on June 27, 1844, the date of the Martyrdom, Brigham Young and Wilford Woodruff spent much of the day

Joseph Smith was martyred in the Carthage Jail while serving as mayor of Nauvoo and running for President of the United States.

together. In the evening, while sitting in the railroad station, Elder Young was overcome with a "heavy depression." He was so melancholy that he "could not converse with any degree of pleasure." After the fact he recorded, "Not knowing anything concerning [Joseph Smith's death] at this time in Carthage Jail, I could not assign my reasons for my peculiar feelings."[248] It would be nearly two weeks before the Apostles in New England would receive word that the Prophet had been martyred. Therefore, they diligently continued to campaign for Joseph Smith even though he had already died.

The Massachusetts Convention and the New England States

The most significant political gathering in behalf of Joseph Smith outside of Nauvoo took place in Boston four days after the Prophet had been killed. At least six Apostles attended that event: Brigham Young, Orson Hyde, William Smith, Orson Pratt, Wilford Woodruff, and Lyman Wight.

These Apostles and many others began to gather in Boston during the last week of June for a large Church conference followed by the state political convention in behalf of the Prophet. Brigham Young had arrived in Boston on June 16 and had been in or near the city ever since. Wilford Woodruff had come from Albany on June 26. During the next two days, Heber C. Kimball, Orson Hyde, William Smith, Orson Pratt, and Lyman Wight all came to Boston from other cities in the East but outside New England.

First the Apostles held a Church conference in Franklin Hall on June 29 and 30. Brigham Young presided, and seven members of the Twelve attended. Orson Hyde spoke in the Saturday morning session "in a very interesting manner." Brigham Young, Heber C. Kimball, and Lyman Wight each addressed the assembly in the afternoon session. Elders Young and Kimball also ordained two elders during the meeting.[249]

The following day, Orson Pratt spoke in the morning session and "took away all the objections of the world against new revelation." Lyman Wight spoke again in the afternoon meeting on a wide variety of subjects, including "the immortality of the body as well as the soul," baptism for the dead, and charity. In the evening session, Wilford Woodruff spoke on the topic "Ye are my friends if ye do whatsoever I command you." The Twelve seemed pleased with the meetings. "The house was full through the day and evening," wrote Woodruff, "and much instruction was given . . . during the whole Conference by those who spoke."[250]

The next day, July 1, they held their political convention. The Twelve had already participated in numerous political meetings in May and June, but, in some respects, this one was different. It was the first political rally held in New England, the ancestral home of many leaders and members from the early days of the restored Church.

In addition, this was more than just another local political rally or mass meeting. This gathering was an official state convention for Joseph Smith's independent political party, which would elect delegates to a national convention to be held in Baltimore on July 13, 1844.[251] The only other state convention that had been held for Joseph Smith's party had been in Nauvoo on May 17, 1844.[252] Finally, this convention was attended by at least six members of the Quorum of Twelve Apostles, which was twice as many as had attended any other political rally for the Prophet outside of Nauvoo.

The convention was held at the Melodeon, a public hall on Washington Street "between the paramount theatre on the south and the opera house on the north."[253] The meeting began at 10 A.M. Brigham Young was president of the convention, and William Smith and Lyman Wight served as vice presidents. The assembly formally nominated Joseph Smith as candidate for president of the United States and Sidney Rigdon as vice president. Speakers included Brigham Young, Orson Hyde, William Smith, Orson Pratt, and Lyman Wight of the Quorum of the Twelve Apostles and George B. Wallace of Boston. "The convention was addressed with much animation and zeal," declared Wilford Woodruff, and it was "attended with sound argument during the day and evening."[254]

Unfortunately, some serious disruptions occurred. "The Melodeon was [crowded] in the evening and it was soon evident that a large number of rowdies were in the galleries & felt disposed to make [a] disturbance."[255] In the middle of Brigham Young's talk, a woman named Abby Folsom rudely rose from her seat and began speaking. Soon thereafter an unruly young man stood and started yelling mean-spirited remarks from the gallery, all the while being encouraged by his raucous companions.

Ultimately, chaos broke out in the gallery, and the police had to be summoned to escort the young man out of the building. The law enforcement officers "were assaulted and beaten badly by a set of young desperadoes."[256] One person was cut badly on his face. After a considerable amount of fighting, however, the gallery was finally cleared. Wilford Woodruff called the disruption "a disgrace to Boston and shows the spirit of the times."[257] Brigham Young proclaimed, "This proves that the voice of the people rules: that, is the voice of the rabble."[258] Nonetheless, before the convention broke up, the Elders accomplished some important business: they officially nominated Heber C. Kimball and S. B. Wallace as delegates to the national convention in Baltimore.[259]

Despite the disruptions at the Boston convention, the Apostles remained optimistic. Wilford Woodruff claimed, "The citizens [could] see [there] was sufficient reason to awaken the minds of the people upon the affairs of our government, in order to save them from ruin."[260] In addition, Brigham Young wrote that "all of this did us good in Boston."[261] The convention received enough attention that the *Boston Daily Times* published its proceedings.[262]

On July 2, the Twelve met with the elders in the area at Franklin Hall. At this meeting they decided "to divide into different parts of the vineyard; each one of the Twelve was appointed to take the oversight of several conferences."[263] Then they all went to a nearby home and administered to William Smith's wife, who was ill.[264] At 4 P.M. Lyman Wight gave a political address at Bunker Hill.[265] At 7 P.M. Wilford Woodruff left Boston for Portland, Maine. Four days later he presided at a conference in Scarboro, Maine.[266]

On the evening of the Fourth of July, Brigham Young, Heber C. Kimball, and other members of the Twelve attended "a grand exhibition of fireworks on the Boston common."[267] Then, by July 7, Elders Kimball, Pratt, and Wight were all participating in a conference in Salem, Massachusetts.[268]

July 9, 1844, was truly significant in the lives of five of the Latter-day Saint Apostles serving in New England. On that day they heard rumors of the tragic death of their beloved prophet, Joseph Smith. Brigham Young and Orson Pratt were in Boston when they received word of the Martyrdom, but they did not want to believe it. Heber C. Kimball and Lyman Wight were still in Salem when they heard of the killing. They immediately left for Boston to be with Brigham and Orson.[269] Wilford Woodruff was in Portland, Maine, getting ready to take a steamboat to the Fox Islands. After reading an account of the Martyrdom in the *Boston Times,* he immediately changed his plans to go to the islands and the next day took a train to Boston.[270]

For the next week or so these five Apostles attempted to carry on the work of the Church in the East until they received sure word that the Prophet had been killed. On July 16, while staying in Boston, Wilford Woodruff received two letters from Nauvoo confirming Joseph's death. He then wrote a letter to Brigham Young, validating the news of the Martyrdom.[271]

Brigham Young and Orson Pratt were in Peterboro,

New Hampshire, participating in a Church conference when Brigham received Wilford's letter. Earlier in the day, Elders Young and Pratt had another letter read to them about the Prophet's death. Brigham Young wrote about his reaction: "The first thing which I thought of was, whether Joseph had taken the keys of the kingdom with him from the earth; brother Orson Pratt sat on my left; we were both leaning back on our chairs. Bringing my hand down to my knee, I said the keys of the kingdom are right here with the Church."[272] Brigham started back to Boston that evening.

Elder Young arrived in Boston the next day, July 17. He and Wilford Woodruff walked to the house of Sister Voce, who lived at 57 Temple Street. Here emotion finally overcame these two great Apostles as they expressed their sadness at the death of Joseph Smith. Elder Woodruff recorded, "[Brother] Young took the bed and I the big chair, and I here veiled my face and for the first time gave vent to my grief and mourning for . . . Joseph and [Hyrum] Smith who were murdered by a gentile mob. After being bathed by a flood of tears I felt composed."[273]

On July 18, Brigham Young, Heber C. Kimball, Orson Hyde, Orson Pratt, and Wilford Woodruff met in Boston and made plans to return to Nauvoo. They wrote an open letter "To the Elders and Saints Scattered Abroad" and had it published in the Church periodical *The Prophet*. In this epistle they admonished all the brethren who had families in the West to "return to them as soon as convenient."[274] That night Orson Hyde and Brigham Young spoke to members and friends in a hall on Washington Street in Boston.[275] The Apostles stayed in the East for another six days, preaching the gospel, taking care of Church business, and bidding farewell to friends and relatives. On July 24, Elders Young, Kimball, Hyde, Pratt, Woodruff, and Wight departed for Nauvoo.

Conclusion

The campaign of the Twelve Apostles for Joseph Smith was a fascinating episode in Church history. It was unique inasmuch as the Apostles were called as "electioneer" missionaries to both proselytize for the Church and campaign for the Prophet. The Twelve also scheduled Church conferences all over the United States. Political rallies were often scheduled either the day before or the day after these conferences. The Apostles tried to visit as many of the conferences as possible.

One scholar has observed that "while many electioneers gave political addresses and distributed copies of Joseph Smith's platform, in the main, their activities did more to strengthen the Church than to present the Prophet to the nation as a presidential candidate."[276] A careful analysis of the missionary activities of the Twelve makes it evident that the Apostles also expended more energy in building the ecclesiastical kingdom than in campaigning for Joseph.

For example, Wilford Woodruff's electioneer mission lasted about nine weeks. During that time he was involved in only five political meetings, averaging one every twelve days. Brigham Young's mission lasted approximately seven weeks. He gave five political addresses during that time—about one every eight days. Both Apostles spent at least twice as much time in Church meetings as they did in political rallies. Nevertheless, it is significant that these two great missionaries each spoke in at least five political gatherings during a period of just seven to nine weeks.

Historians have written much about how certain events in Church history helped prepared the Twelve, especially Brigham Young, to one day lead the Church. Zion's Camp, the expulsion of the Mormons from Missouri, and the mission of the Twelve to the British Isles are all episodes that provided the Apostles with significant leadership opportunities.[277] Certainly another important event that should be added to that list is the involvement of the Twelve in Joseph Smith's campaign for president.

Scholars often overlook the fact that the Apostles who campaigned in the eastern United States collectively visited members in the nation's capital and nearly half the states of the Union during the two months preceding Joseph Smith's death. This experience also helped prepare them to "bear off the kingdom"[278] after the martyrdom of their prophet.

Epilogue

Was Joseph Smith a Serious Candidate for President?

Occasionally people ask whether Joseph Smith considered himself a serious candidate for president. The venerable B. H. Roberts gave the traditional view: "Of course President Smith could have no hope that he would be elected to the presidency," and he "usually referred to his candidacy in a jocular vein."[279] Roberts justified his position by quoting the Prophet's statement: "I care but little about the presidential chair. I would not give half as much for the office of President of the United States as I would for . . . Lieutenant-General of the Nauvoo Legion."[280]

Recently, historians have argued that Joseph's campaign was much more serious than Roberts would have us believe. To support this view they cite a talk the Prophet gave on January 29, 1844: "If I ever get into the presidential chair, I will protect the people in their rights and liberties. . . . There is oratory enough in the Church to carry me into the presidential chair the first slide."[281] Also, on February 8, he said, "I feel it to be my right and privilege to obtain what influence and power I can, lawfully, in the United States for the protection of injured innocence."[282] Joseph then went on to speculate that he might be killed because of the campaign. These are hardly the words of a frivolous candidate.

There is also evidence that Joseph Smith's enemies were serious about the Prophet's campaign. The *History of the Church* tells of a meeting wherein Joseph Smith's antagonists plotted to kill him for political reasons. They were concerned that Joseph's "views on government were widely circulated and took like wildfire."[283] According to a Dr. Southwick, who attended the meeting, they believed that if the Prophet "did not get in the presidential chair this election, he would be sure to next time; and if Illinois and Missouri would join together and kill him, they would not be brought to justice for it."[284] According to Southwick, "There were delegates in said meeting from every state in the Union except three."[285] If this account is accurate, it leads one to believe that the Prophet's campaign was at least one cause of his death. Indeed, entire books have recently been written about this subject.[286]

In 1973, James B. Allen wrote a brief article in the *Ensign* magazine concerning the seriousness of Joseph Smith's campaign. He acknowledges that the subject is "still a matter of debate even among Church historians."[287] Dr. Allen believes that the Prophet did not think he could win the presidency, but "he was serious in attempting to influence public opinion by using every possible means to promote his own political views."[288]

It would seem, therefore, that if the Prophet directed Church leaders to call more than three hundred men to campaign in every state of the Union and organize forty-seven conferences in fifteen different states, then he was absolutely serious about influencing public opinion, especially regarding the powers of the president of the United States. The fact that at least forty-five newspapers in twenty-two states published articles about Joseph Smith's campaign suggests that the Prophet was, indeed, having some influence on public opinion. In addition, because so many editors chose to publish articles about Joseph Smith's campaign indicates that numerous newspapers took his campaign seriously.

There is an important corollary to the question, however, that has seldom, if ever, been addressed. It concerns the attitude of high-ranking leaders of the Church. Specifically, how serious were the Apostles and Hyrum Smith about the Prophet's campaign? A brief recitation of some of their remarks leads to the conclusion that they were undeniably serious about the candidacy.

Willard Richards admonished the Apostles and other leaders to "use all honorable means in [their] power to secure [the Prophet's] election."[289] Richards also referred to Joseph Smith as "the greatest statesman of the 19th century."[290] Upon encouraging one brother to become involved in the campaign, he said, "If you act well your part, victory's the prize."[291]

On one occasion Brigham Young stated, "We are acquainted with the views of Gen. Smith, the Democrats and Whigs and all factions. It is now time to have a President of the United States. Elders will be sent to preach the gospel and electioneer."[292] To this Hyrum Smith added, "Lift up your voices like thunder: there is power and influence enough among us to put in a President."[293]

On April 8, Heber C. Kimball affirmed, "We design to send Elders to all the different States to get up meetings and protracted meetings, and electioneer for Joseph to be the next President."[294] Finally, on May 18, Elder George A. Smith spoke to a large political rally with several hundred citizens assembled. He declared that General Smith was "the smartest man in the United States, and best calculated to fill the presidential chair."[295] Skeptics might dismiss the above comments as political rhetoric but, if we are to take these men at their word, it is difficult to believe that they were anything less than serious about the campaign.

Of course, we will never be able to measure how much influence Joseph Smith might have had on the 1844 presidential campaign. However, when we consider his campaign, we are reminded of a statement by Edmund Burke: "All that is necessary for the triumph of evil is for good men to do nothing."[296] To this, President Ezra Taft Benson has said, "It is not enough that we wring our hands and moan about conditions in America. We must become . . . 'anxiously engaged' in good causes and leave the world a better place for having lived in it."[297]

Joseph Smith literally gave his life to make the world a better place in which to live—both spiritually and politically.

Appendix A: Correspondence between Joseph Smith and John C. Calhoun

Joseph Smith's Letter to John C. Calhoun

Hon. John C. Calhoun,

DEAR SIR,—As we understand you are a candidate for the Presidency at the next election; and as the Latter-day Saints (sometimes called "Mormons," who now constitute a numerous class in the school politic of this vast republic,) have been robbed of an immense amount of property, and endured nameless sufferings by the State of Missouri, and from her borders have been driven by force of arms, contrary to our national covenants; and as in vain we have sought redress by all constitutional, legal, and honorable means, in her courts, her executive councils, and her legislative halls; and as we have petitioned Congress to take cognizance of our sufferings without effect, we have judged it wisdom to address you this communication, and solicit an immediate, specific, and candid reply to "What will be your rule of action relative to us as a people," should fortune favor your ascension to the chief magistracy?

Most respectfully, sir, your friend,
and the friend of peace, good order,
and constitutional rights,

JOSEPH SMITH

In behalf of the Church of Jesus Christ of Latter-day Saints.

Letter: John C. Calhoun to Joseph Smith—Defining What Former's Policy would be Towards the Saints if Elected President.

FORT HILL, December 2, 1843.

Sir:—You ask me what would be my rule of action relative the Mormons of Latter-day Saints, should I be elected President; to which I answer, that if I should be elected, I would strive to administer the government according to the Constitution and the laws of the union; and that as they make no distinction between citizens of different religious creeds I should make none. As far as it depends on the Executive department, all should have the full benefit of both, and none should be exempt from their operation.

But as you refer to the case of Missouri, candor compels me to repeat what I said to you at Washington, that, according to my views, the case does not come within the jurisdiction of the Federal Government, which is one of limited and specific powers.

With respect, I am, &c, &c.,

J. C. CALHOUN.

Letter: Joseph Smith to John C. Calhoun—The Latter's Policy Towards the Latter-day Saints, if Elected President of the U.S. Considered.

NAUVOO, ILLINOIS, January 2, 1844.

Sir:—Your reply to my letter of last November, concerning your rule of action towards the Latter-day Saints, if elected President, is at land; and that you and your friends of the same opinion relative to the matter in question may not be disappointed as to me or my mind upon so grave a subject, permit me, as a law-abiding man, as a well-wisher to the perpetuity of constitutional rights and liberty, and as a friend to the free worship of Almighty God by all, according to the dictates of every person's own conscience, to say that *I am surprised* that a man or men in the highest stations of public life should have made up such a fragile "view" of a case, than which there is not one of the face of the globe fraught with so much consequence to the happiness of men in this world or the world to come.

To be sure, the first paragraph of your letter appears very complacent and fair on a white sheet of paper. And who, that is ambitious for greatness and power, would not have said the same thing? Your oath binds you to support the Constitution and laws; and as all creeds and religions are alike tolerated, they must, of course, all be justified or condemned according to merit or demerit. But why—tell me why are all the principal men held up for public stations *so cautiously careful* not to publish to the world that they will *judge a righteous judgment, law or no law?* For laws and opinions, like the vanes of steeples, change with the wind.

One Congress passes a law, another repeals it; and one statesman say that the Constitution means this, and another that; and who does not know that all may be wrong? The opinion and pledge, therefore, in the first paragraph of your reply to my question, like the forced steam from the engine of a steam-boat, makes the shod of a bright cloud at first; but when it comes in contact with a purer atmosphere, dissolved to common air again.

Your second paragraph leaves you naked before yourself, like a likeness in a mirror, when you say, that according to your *view*, the Federal Government is "one of limited and specific powers," and has no jurisdiction in the case of the "Mormons."

So then a State can at any time expel any portion of her citizens with impunity: and, in the language of Mr. Van Buren, frosted over with your gracious "*views of the case*," though the cause is ever so just, Government can do nothing for them, because it has no power.

Go on, then, Missouri, after another set of inhabitants (as the Latter-day Saints did,) have entered some two or three hundred thousand dollars' worth of land, and made extensive improvements thereon; go on, then, I say; banish the occupants or owners, or kill them, as the mobbers did many of the Latter-day Saints, and take their land and property as spoil; and let the Legislature, as in the case of the "Mormons," appropriate a couple of hundred thousand dollars to pay the mob for doing that job; for the renowned Senator from South Carolina, Mr. J. C. Calhoun, says the powers of the Federal Government are so *specific and limited that it has no jurisdiction of the case!* O ye people who groan under the oppression of tyrants!—ye exiled Poles, who have felt the iron hand of Russian grasp!—ye poor and unfortunate among all nations! Come to the asylum of the oppressed; buy ye lands of the General Government; pay in your money to the treasury to strengthen the army and the navy; worship God according to the dictates of your own consciences; pay in your taxes to support the great heads of a glorious nation: but remember a "*sovereign State*" is so much more powerful than the United States, the parent Government, that it can exile you at pleasure, mob you with impunity, confiscate your lands and property, have the Legislature sanction it,—yea, even murder you as an edict of an emperor, *and it does no wrong*; for the noble Senator of South Carolina says the power of the federal Government is *so limited and specific, that it has no jurisdiction of the case*! What think ye of *imperium in imperio?*

Ye spirits of the blessed of all ages, hark! Ye shades of departed statesmen, listen! Abraham, Moses, Homer, Socrates, Solon, Solomon, and all that ever thought of right and wrong, look down from your exaltations if you have any; for it is said, "In the midst of counselors there is *safety*;" and when you have learned that fifteen thousand innocent citizens, after having purchased their lands of the United States and paid for them, were expelled from a "sovereign State," by order of the Governor, at the point of the bayonet, their arms taken from them by the same authority, and their right of migration into said State denied, under pain of imprisonment, whipping, robbing, mobbing, and even death, and no justice or recompense allowed; and, from the Legislature with the Governor at the head, down to the Justice of the Peace, with a bottle of whisky in one hand and a bowie-knife in the other, hear them all declare that there is no justice for a "Mormon" in that State; and judge ye a righteous judgment, and tell me when the virtue of the States was stolen, where the honor of the General Government lies hid, and what clothes a senator with wisdom. O nullifying Carolina! O little tempestuous Rhode Island! Would it not be well for the great men of the nation to read the fable of the *partial judge;* and when part of the free citizens of a State had been expelled contrary to the Constitution, mobbed, robbed, plundered, and many murdered, instead of searching into the course taken with Joanna Southcott, Ann Lee, the French Prophets, the Quakers of New England, and rebellious negroes in the slave States, to hear both sides and then judge, rather than have the mortification to say, "Oh, it is *my* bill that has killed *your* ox! That alters the case! I must inquire into it; *and if, and if—!*

If the General Government has no power to reinstate expelled citizens to their rights, there is a monstrous hypocrite fed and fostered from the hard earnings of the people! A real "bull beggar" upheld by sycophants. And although you may wink to the priest to stigmatize, wheedle the drunkards to swear, and raise the hue-and-cry of—"Impostor! False prophet! G—d—n old Joe Smith!" yet remember, if the Latter-day Saints are not restored to all their rights and paid for all their losses, according to the known rules of justice and judgment, reciprocation and common honesty among men, that God will come out of His hiding place, and vex this nation with a sore vexation: yea, the consuming wrath of an offended God shall smoke through the nation with as much distress and woe as independence has blazed through with pleasure and delight. Where is the strength of Government? Where is the patriotism of a Washington, a Warren, an Adams? And where is a spark from the watch-fire of '76, by which one candle might be lit that would glimmer upon the confines of Democracy? Well may it be said that one man is not a state, nor one state a nation.

In the days of General Jackson, when France refused the first installment for spoliations, there was power, force, and honor enough to resent injustice and insult, and the money came; and shall Missouri, filled with negro-drivers and white men stealers, go "unwhipped of justice" for tenfold greater sins than France? No! verily, no! While I have powers of body and mind—while water runs and grass grows—while virtue is lovely and vice hateful; and while a stone points out a sacred spot where a fragment of American liberty once was, I or my posterity will plead the cause of injured innocence, until Missouri makes atonement for all her sins, or sinks disgraced, degraded, and damned to hell, "where the worm dieth not, and the fire is not quenched."

Why, sir, the powers not delegated to the United States and the States belong to the people, and Congress sent to do the people's business have all power; and shall fifteen thousand citizens groan in exile? O vain men! will yet not, if ye do not restore them to their rights and $2,000,000 worth of property, relinquish to them, (the Latter-day Saints,) as a body, their portion of power that belongs to them according to the Constitution? Power has its convenience as well as inconvenience. "The world was not made for Caesar alone, but for Cassius too."

I will give you a parable. A certain lord had a vineyard in a goodly land, which men labored in at their pleasure. A few meek men also went and purchased with money from some of these chief men that labored at pleasure a portion of land in the vineyard, at a very remote part of it, and began to improve it, and to eat and drink the fruit thereof,—when some vile persons, who regarded not man, neither feared the lord of the vineyard, rose up suddenly and robbed these meek men, and drove them from their possessions, killing many.

This barbarous act made no small stir among the men in the vineyard; and all that portion who were attached to that part of the vineyard where the men were robbed rose up in grand council, with their chief man, who had firstly ordered the deed to be done, and made a covenant not to pay for the cruel deed, but to keep the spoil, and never let those meek men set their feet on that soil again, neither recompense them for it.

Now, these meek men, in their distress, wisely sought redress of those wicked men in every possible manner, and got none. They then supplicated the chief men, who held the vineyard at pleasure, and who had the power to sell and defend it, for redress and redemption; and those men, loving the fame and favor of the multitude more than the glory of the lord of the vineyard, answered—"Your cause is just but we can do nothing for you, because we have no power."

Now, when the lord of the vineyard saw that virtue and innocence were not regarded, and his vineyard occupied by wicked men, he sent men and took the possession of it to himself, and destroyed those unfaithful servants, and appointed them their portion among hypocrites.

And let me say that all men who say that Congress has no power to restore and defend the rights of her citizens have not the love of the truth abiding in them. Congress has power to protect the nation against foreign invasion and internal broil; and whenever that body passes an act to maintain right with any power, or to restore right to any portion of her citizens, it is the *supreme law of the land*; and should a State refuse submission, that State is guilty of *insurrection or rebellion*, and the President has as much power to repel it as Washington had to march against the "whisky boys at Pittsburg," or General Jackson had to send an armed force to suppress the rebellion of South Carolina.

To close, I would admonish you, before you let your "*candor compel*" you again to write upon a subject great as the salvation of man, consequential as the life of the Savior, broad as the principles of eternal truth, and valuable as the jewels of eternity, to read in the 8th section and 1st article of the Constitution of the United States, the *first, fourteenth* and *seventeenth* "specific" and not very "limited powers" of the Federal Government, what can be done to protect the lives, property, and rights of a virtuous people, when the administrators of the law and law-makers are unbought by bribes, uncorrupted by patronage, untempted by gold, unawed by fear, and uncontaminated by tangling alliances—even like Caesar's wife, not only *unspotted, but unsuspected!* And God, who cooled the heat of a Nebuchadnezzar's furnace or shut the mouths of lions for the honor of a Daniel, will raise your mind above the narrow notion that the General Government has no power, to the sublime idea that Congress, with the President as Executor, is as almighty in its sphere as Jehovah is in his.

With great respect, I have the honour to be

Your obedient servant,

JOSEPH SMITH.

Source: *History of the Church*, 6:64, 155–60

Appendix B: *General Smith's Views of the Powers and Policy of the Government of the United States*

Born in a land of liberty, and breathing an air uncorrupted with the sirocco of barbarous climes, I ever feel a double anxiety for the happiness of all men, both in time and in eternity.

My cogitations, like Daniel's, have for a long time troubled me, when I viewed the condition of men throughout the world, and more especially in this boasted realm, where the Declaration of Independence "holds these truths to be self-evident, that all men are created equal; that they are endowed by their Creator with certain unalienable rights; that among these are life, liberty, and the pursuit of happiness;" but at the same time some two or three millions of people are held as slaves for life, because the spirit in them is covered with a darker skin than ours; and hundreds of our own kindred for an infraction, or supposed infraction, of some over-wise statute, have to be incarcerated in dungeon gloom, or penitentiaries, while the duelist, the debauchee, and the defaulter for millions, and other criminals, take the uppermost rooms at feasts, or, like the bird of passage, find a more congenial clime by flight.

This wisdom which ought to characterize the freest, wisest, and most noble nation of the nineteenth century, should like the sun in his meridian splendor, warm every object beneath its rays; and the main efforts of her officers, who are nothing more nor less than the servants of the people, ought to be directed to ameliorate the condition of all, black or white, bond or free; for the best of books says, "God hath made of one blood all nations of men for to dwell on all the face of the earth."

Our common country presents to all men the same advantages, the facilities, the same prospects, the same honors, and the same rewards; and without hypocrisy, the Constitution, when it says, "We, the people of the United States, in order to form a more perfect union, establish justice, ensure domestic tranquility, provide for the common defense, promote the general welfare, and secure the blessings of liberty to ourselves and our posterity, do ordain and establish this Constitution for the United States of America," meant just what it said without reference to color or condition, *ad infinitum*.

The aspirations and expectations of a virtuous people, environed with so wise, so liberal, so deep, so broad, and so high a charter of *equal rights* as appears in said Constitution, ought to be treated by those to whom the administration of the laws is entrusted with as much sanctity as the prayers of the Saints are treated in heaven, that love, confidence, and union, like the sun, moon, and stars should bear witness,

"For ever singing as they shine.
The hand that made us is divine!"

Unity is power; and when I reflect on the importance of it to the stability of all governments, I am astounded at the silly moves of persons and parties to foment discord in order to ride into power on the current popular excitement; nor am I less surprised at the stretches of power or restrictions of right which too often appear as acts of legislators to pave the way to some favorite political scheme as destitute of intrinsic merit as a wolf's heart is of the mild of human kindness. A Frenchman would say, *"Presque tout aimer richesses et pouvoir."* (Almost all men like wealth and power.)

I must dwell on this subject longer than others; for nearly

one hundred years ago that golden patriot, Benjamin Franklin, drew up a plan of union for the then colonies of Great Britain, that *now* are such an independent nation, which, among many wise provisions for obedient children under their father's more rugged hand, had this:—"They have power to make laws, and lay and levy such general duties, imports, or taxes as to them shall appear most equal and just, (considering the ability and other circumstances of the inhabitants in the several colonies,) and such as may be collected with the least inconvenience to the people, rather discouraging luxury than loading industry with unnecessary burthens." Great Britain surely lacked the laudable humanity and fostering clemency to grant such a just plan of union; but the sentiment remains, like the land that honored its birth, as a pattern for wise men *to study the convenience of the people more than the comfort of the cabinet.*

And one of the most noble fathers of our freedom and country's glory, great in war, great in peace, great in the estimation of the world, and great in the hears of his countrymen, (the illustrious Washington,) said in his first inaugural address to Congress—"I behold the surest pledges that as, on one side, no local prejudices or attachments, no separate views or party animosities will misdirect the comprehensive and equal eye which ought to watch over this great assemblage of communities and interests, so, on another, that the foundations of our national policy will be laid in the pure and immutable principles of private morality, and the pre-eminence of free government be exemplified by all the attributes which can win the affections of its citizens and command the respect of the world."

Verily, here shine the virtue and wisdom of a statesman in such lucid rays, that had every succeeding Congress followed the rich instruction in all their deliberations and enactments, for the benefit and convenience of the whole community and the communities of which it is composed, no sound of a rebellion in South Carolina, no rupture in Rhode Island, no mob in Missouri expelling her citizens by Executive authority, corruption in the ballot-boxes, a border warfare between Ohio and Michigan, hard times and distress, outbreak upon outbreak in the principal cities, murder, robbery, and defalcation, scarcity of money, and a thousand other difficulties, would have torn asunder the bonds of the Union, destroyed the confidence of man with man, and left the great body of the people to mourn over misfortunes in poverty brought on by corrupt legislation in an hour of proud vanity for self-aggrandizement.

The great Washington, soon after the foregoing faithful admonition for the common welfare of his nation, further advised Congress that "among the many interesting objects which will engage your attention, that of providing for the common defense will merit particular regard. To be prepared for war is one of the most effectual means of preserving peace." As the Italian would say—"*Buono aviso.*"

The elder Adams, in his inaugural address, gives national pride such a grand turn of justification, that every honest citizen must look back upon the infancy of the United States with an approving smile, and rejoice that patriotism in their rulers, virtue in the people, and prosperity in the Union once crowded the expectations of hope, unveiled the sophistry of the hypocrite, and silenced the folly of foes. Mr. Adams said, "If national pride is ever justifiable or excusable, it is when it springs not from *power* or riches, grandeur or glory, but from conviction of national innocence information, and benevolence."

There is no doubt such was actually the case with our young realm at the close of the last century. Peace, prosperity, and union filled the country with religious toleration, temporal enjoyment, and virtuous enterprise; and grandly, too, when the deadly winter of the "Stamp Act," the "Tea Act," and other close communion acts of Royalty had choked the growth of freedom of speech, liberty of the press, and liberty of conscience—did light, liberty, and loyalty flourish like the cedars of God.

The respected and venerable Thomas Jefferson, in his inaugural address, made more than forty years ago, shows what a beautiful prospect an innocent, virtuous nation presents to the sage's eye, where there is space for enterprise, hands for industry, heads for heroes, and hearts for moral greatness. He said, "A rising nation spread over a wide and fruitful land, traversing all the seas with the rich productions of their industry, engaged in commerce with nations who feel power and forget right, advancing rapidly to destinies beyond the reach of mortal eye,—when I contemplate these transcendent objects, and see the honor, the happiness, and the hopes of this beloved country committed to the issue and the auspices of this day, I shrink from the contemplation, and humble myself before the magnitude of the undertaking."

Such a prospect was truly soul-stirring to a good man. But "since the fathers have fallen asleep," wicked and designing men have unrobed the Government of its glory; and the people, if not in dust and ashes, or in sackcloth, have to lament in poverty her departed greatness, while demagogues build fires in the north and south, east and west, to keep up their spirits *till it is better times.* But year after year has left the people to *hope*, till the very name of *Congress* or *State Legislature* is as horrible to the sensitive friend of his country as the house of "Bluebard" is to children, or "Crockford's" Hell of London to meek men.[298]

When the people are secure and their rights properly respected, then the four main pillars of prosperity—viz., agriculture, manufactures, navigation, and commerce, need the fostering care of Government; and in so goodly a country as ours, where the soil, the climate, the rivers, the lakes, and the sea coast, the productions, the timber, the minerals, and the inhabitants are so diversified, that a pleasing variety accommodates all tastes, trades, and calculations, it certainly is the highest point of supervision to protect the whole northern and southern, eastern and western, centre and circumference of the realm, by a judicious tariff. It is an old saying and a true one, "If you wish to be *respected*, respect yourselves."

I will adopt in part the language of Mr. Madison's inaugural address,—"To cherish peace and friendly intercourse with all nations, having correspondent dispositions; to maintain sincere neutrality towards belligerent nations; to prefer in all cases amicable discussion and reasonable accommodation of differences to a decision of them by an appeal to arms; to exclude foreign intrigues and foreign partialities, so degrading to all counties, and so baneful to free ones; to foster a spirit of independence too just to invade the rights of others, too proud to surrender our own, to liberal to indulge unworthy prejudices ourselves, and too elevated not to look down upon them in others; to hold the union of the States as the basis of their peace and happiness; to support the Constitution, which is the cement of the Union, as well in its limitations as in its authorities; to respect the rights and authorities reserved to the States and to the people as equally incorporated with and essential to the success of the general system; to avoid the slightest interference with the rights of conscience or the functions of religion, so wisely exempted from civil jurisdiction; to preserve in their full energy the other salutary provisions in behalf of private and personal rights, and of the freedom of the press,—so far as intention aids in the fulfillment of duty, are consummations too big with benefits not to captivate the energies of all honest men to achieve them, when they can be brought to pass by reciprocation, friendly alliances, wise legislation, and honorable treaties."

The Government has once flourished under the guidance of trusty servants; and the Hon. Mr. Monroe, in his day, while speaking of the Constitution, says, "Our commerce has been wisely regulated with foreign nations and between the States. New States have been admitted into our Union. Our Territory has been enlarged by fair and honorable treaty, and with great advantage to the original States; the States respectively protected by the national Government, under a mild paternal system against foreign dangers, and enjoying within their separate spheres, by a wise partition of power, a just proportion of the sovereignty, have improved their police, extended their settlements, and attained a strength and maturity which are the best proofs of wholesome laws well administered. And if we look to the condition of individuals, what a proud spectacle does it exhibit! On whom has oppression fallen in any quarter of our Union? Who has been deprived of any right of person or property?—who restrained from offering his vows in the mode which he prefers to the Divine Author of his being? It is well known that all these blessings have been enjoyed in their fullest extent; and I add, with peculiar satisfaction, that there has been no example of a capital punishment being inflicted on any one for the crime of high treason." What a delightful picture of power, policy and prosperity! Truly the wise man's proverb is just—Righteousness exalteth a nation, but sin is a reproach to any people.

But this is not all. The same honorable statesman, after having had about forty years' experience in the Government, under the full tide of successful experiment, gives the following commendatory assurance of the efficiency of the *Magna Charta* to answer its great end and aim—*to protect the people in their rights*. "Such, then, is the happy Government under which we live; a Government adequate to every purpose for which the social compact is formed; a Government elective in all its branches, under which every citizen may by his merit obtain the highest trust recognized by the Constitution, which contains within it no cause of discord, none to put at variance one portion of the community with another; a Government which protests every citizen in the full enjoyment of his rights, and is able to protect the nation against injustice from foreign powers."

Again, the younger Adams, in the silver age of our country's advancement to fame, in his inaugural address (1825), thus candidly declares the majesty of the youthful republic in its increasing greatness:—"The year of jubilee, since the first formation of our union, has just elapsed: that of the Declaration of Independence is at hand. The consummation of both was effected by this Constitution. Since that period, a population of four millions has multiplied to twelve. A Territory, bounded by the Mississippi, has been extended from sea to sea. New States have been admitted to the Union, in numbers nearly equal to those of the first confederation. Treaties of peace, amity, and commerce have been concluded with the principal dominions of the earth. The people of other nations, the inhabitants of regions acquired, not by conquest, but by compact, have been united with us in the participation of our rights and duties, of our burdens and blessings. The forest has fallen by the ax of our woodsman. The soil has been made to teem by the tillage of our farmers. Our commerce has whitened every ocean. The dominion of man over physical nature has been extended by the invention of our artists. Liberty and law have marched hand in hand. All the purposes of human association have been accomplished as effectively as under any other Government on the globe, and at a cost little exceeding, in a whole generation, the expenditures of other nations in a single year."

In continuation of such noble sentiments, General Jackson, upon his ascension to the great chair of the chief magistracy, said, "As long as our Government is administered for the good of the people, and is regulated by their will, as long as it secures to us the rights of person and property, liberty of conscience, and of the press, it will be worth defending; and so long as it is worth defending, a patriotic militia will cover it with an impenetrable *ægis*."

General Jackson's administration may be denominated by the *acme* of American glory, liberty, and prosperity; for the national debt, which in 1815, on account of the late war, was $125,000,000, and being lessened gradually, was paid up in his golden day, and preparations were made to distribute the surplus revenue among the several States; and that august patriot, to use his own words in his farewell address, retired, leaving "a great people prosperous and happy, in the full enjoyment of liberty and peace, honored and respected by every nation of the world."

At the age, then, of sixty years, our blooming Republic began to decline under the withering touch of Martin Van Buren! Disappointed ambition, thirst for power, pride, corruption, party spirit, faction, patronage, perquisites, fame, tangling alliances, priestcraft, and spiritual wickedness in *high places*, struck hands and reveled in midnight splendor.

Trouble, vexation, perplexity, and contention, mingled with hope, fear, and murmuring, rumbled through the Union and agitated the whole nation, as would an earthquake at the centre of the earth, the world heaving the sea beyond its bounds and shaking the everlasting hills; so, in hopes of better times, while jealousy, hypocritical pretensions, and pompous ambition were luxuriating on the ill-gotten spoils of the people, they rose in their majesty like a tornado, and swept through the land, till General Harrison appeared as a star among the storm-clouds for better weather.

The calm came, and the language of that venerable patriot, in his inaugural address, while descanting upon the merits of the Constitution and its framers, thus expressed himself:—

"There were in it features which appeared not to be in harmony with their ideas of a simple representative Democracy or Republic. And knowing the tendency of power to increase itself, particularly when executed by a single individual, predictions were made that, and no very remote period, the Government would terminate in virtual monarchy.

"It would not become me to say that the fears of these patriots have been already realized. But as I sincerely believe that the tendency of measures and of men's opinions for some years past has been in that direction, it is, I conceive, strictly proper that I should take this occasion to repeat the assurances I have heretofore given of my determination to arrest the progress of that tendency, if it really exists, and restore the Government to its pristine health and vigor."

This good man died before he had the opportunity of applying one balm to ease the pain of our groaning country, and I am willing the nation should be the judge, whether General Harrison, in his exalted station, upon the eve of his entrance into the world of spirits, told the truth, or not, with acting President Tyler's three years of perplexity, and pseudo-Whig-Democrat reign to heal the breaches or show the wounds, *secundum artem*.

Subsequent events, all things considered, Van Buren's downfall, Harrison's exit, and Tyler's self-sufficient turn to the whole, go to show*__ * * * * *certainly there is a God in heaven to reveal secrets.*

No honest man can doubt for a moment but the glory of American liberty is on the wane, and that calamity and confusion will sooner or later destroy the peace of the people. Speculators will urge a national bank as a savior of credit and comfort. A hireling pseudo-priesthood will plausibly push abolition doctrines and doings and "human rights" into Congress, and into every other place where conquest smells of fame, or opposition swells to popularity. Democracy, Whiggery, and cliquery will attract their elements and foment divisions among the people, to accomplish fancied schemes and accumulate power, while poverty, driven to despair, like hunger forcing its way through a wall, will break through the statutes of men to save life, and mend the breach in prison glooms.

A still higher grade of what the "nobility of nations" call "great men" will dally with all rights, in order to smuggle a fortune at "one fell swoop," mortgage Texas, possess Oregon, and claim all the unsettled regions of the world for hunting and trapping; and should an humble, honest man, red, black, or white, exhibit a better title, these gentry have only to clothe the judge with richer ermine, and spangle the lawyer's finger with finger rings, to have the judgment of his peers and the honor of his lords as a pattern of honesty, virtue, and humanity, while the motto hangs on his nation's escutcheon—*"Every man has his price!"*

Now, O people! people! turn unto the Lord and live, and reform this nation. Frustrate the designs of wicked men. Reduce Congress at least two-thirds. Two Senators from a State and two members to a million of population will do more business than the army that now occupy the halls of the national Legislature. Pay them two dollars and their board per diem (except Sundays.) That is more than the farmer gets, and he lives honestly. Curtail the officers of Government in pay, number, and power; for the Philistine lords have shorn our nation of its goodly locks in the lap of Delilah.

Petition your State Legislatures to pardon every convict in their several penitentiaries, blessing them as they go, and saying to them, in the name of the Lord, *Go thy way, and sin no more.*

Advise your legislators, when they make laws for larceny, burglary, or any felony, to make the penalty applicable to work upon roads, public works, or any place where the culprit can be taught more wisdom and more virtue, and become more enlightened. Rigor and seclusion will never do as much to reform the propensities of men as reason and friendship. Murder only can claim confinement or death. Let the penitentiaries be turned into seminaries of learning, where intelligence, like the angels of heaven, would banish such fragments of barbarism. Imprisonment for debt is a meaner practice than the savage tolerates, with all his ferocity. *"Amor vincit omnia."*

Petition, also, ye goodly inhabitants of the slave States, your legislators to abolish slavery by the year 1850, or now, and save the abolitionist from reproach and ruin, infamy and shame.

Pray Congress to pay every man a reasonable price for his slaves out of the surplus revenue arising from the sale of public lands, and from the deduction of pay from the members of Congress.

Break off the shackles from the poor black man, and hire him to labor like other human beings; for "an hour of virtuous liberty on earth is worth a whole eternity of bondage." Abolish the practice in the army and navy of trying men by court-martial for desertion. If a solider or marine runs away, send him his wages, with this instruction, that his country will never trust him again; he has forfeited his honor.

Make honor the standard with all men. Be sure that good is rendered for evil in all cases; and the whole nation, like a kingdom of kings and priests, will rise up in righteousness, and be respected as wise and worthy on earth, and as just and holy for heaven, by Jehovah, the Author of perfection.

More economy in the national and state governments would make less taxes among the people; more equality through the cities, towns, and country, would make less distinction among the people; and more honesty and familiarity in societies would make less hypocrisy and flattery in all branches of the community; and open, frank, candid decorum to all men, in this boasted land of liberty, would beget esteem, confidence, union, love; and the neighbor from any state or from any country, of whatever color, clime or tongue, could rejoice when he put his foot on the sacred soil of freedom, and exclaim, The very name of "*American*" is fraught with "*friendship!*" Oh, then, create confidence, restore freedom, break down slavery, banish imprisonment for debt, and be in love, fellowship and peace with all the world! Remember that honesty is not subject to law. The law was made for transgressors. Wherefore a * * * * good name is better than riches.

For the accommodation of the people in every state and territory, let Congress show their wisdom by granting a national bank, with branches in each State and Territory, where the capital stock shall be held by the nation for the Central bank, and by the states and territories for the branches; and whose officers and directors shall be elected yearly by the people, with wages at the rate of two dollars per day for services; which several banks shall never issue any more bills than the amount of capital stock in her vaults and the interest.

The net gain of the Central bank shall be applied to the national revenue, and that of the branches to the states' and territories' revenues. And the bills shall be par throughout the nation, which will mercifully cure that fatal disorder known in cities as *brokerage*, and leave the people's money in their own pockets.

Give every man his constitutional freedom and the president full power to send an army to suppress mobs, and the States authority to repeal and impugn that relic of folly which makes it necessary for the governor of a state to make the demand of the President for troops, in case of invasion or rebellion.

The governor himself may be a mobber; and instead of being punished, as he should be, for murder or treason, he may destroy the very lives, rights, and property he should protect. Like the good Samaritan, send every lawyer as soon as he repents and obeys the ordinances of heaven, to preach the Gospel to the destitute, without purse or scrip, pouring in the oil and the wine. A learned Priesthood is certainly more honorable than "*an hireling clergy.*"

As to the contiguous territories to the United States, wisdom would direct no tangling alliance. Oregon belongs to this government honorably; and when we have the red man's consent, let the Union spread from the east to the west sea; and if Texas petitions Congress to be adopted among the sons of liberty, give her the right hand of fellowship, and refuse not the same friendly grip to Canada and Mexico. And when the right arm of freemen is stretched out in the character of a navy for the protection of rights, commerce, and honor, let the iron eyes of power watch from Maine to Mexico, and from California to Columbia. Thus may union be strengthened, and foreign speculation prevented from opposing broadside to broadside.

Seventy years have done much for this goodly land. They have burst the chains of oppression and monarchy, and multiplied its inhabitants from two to twenty millions, with a proportionate share of knowledge keen enough to circumnavigate the globe, draw the lightning from the clouds, and cope with all the crowned heads of the world.

They why—oh, why will a once flourishing people not arise, phoenix-like over the cinders of Martin Van Buren's power, and over the sinking fragments and smoking ruins of other catamount politicians, and over the windfalls of Benton, Calhoun, Clay, Wright, and a caravan of other equally unfortunate law doctors, and cheerfully help to spread a plaster and bind up the *burnt, bleeding wounds,* of a sore but blessed country?

The Southern people are hospitable and noble. They will

help to rid so *free* a country of every vestige of slavery, whenever they are assured of an equivalent for their property. The country will be full of money and confidence when a National Bank of twenty millions, and a State Bank in every state, with a million or more, gives a tone to monetary matters, and makes a circulation medium as valuable in the purses of a whole community as in the coffers of a speculation banker or broker.

The people may have faults, but they should never be trifled with. I think Mr. Pitt's quotation in the British Parliament of Mr. Prior's couplet for the husband and wife, to apply to the course which the King and ministry of England should pursue to the then colonies of the *now* United States, might be a genuine rule of action for some of the *breath-made* men in high places to use towards the posterity of this noble, daring people:—

> "Be her faults a little blind;
> Be to her virtues very kind."

We have had Democratic President, Whig Presidents, a pseudo-Democratic-Whig President, and now it is time to have a *President of the United States*; and let the people of the whole Union, like the inflexible Romans, whenever they find a *promise* made by a candidate that is not *practiced* as an officer, hurl the miserable sycophant from his exaltation, as God did Nebuchadnezzar, to crop the grass of the field with a beast's heart among the cattle.

Mr. Van Buren said, in his inaugural address, that he went in the Presidential chair the inflexible and uncompromising opponent of every attempt, on the part of Congress, to abolish slavery in the District of Columbia, against the wishes of the slave-holding States, and also with a determination equally decided to resist the slightest interference with it in the States where it exists.

Poor little Matty made this rhapsodical sweep with the fact before his eyes, that the State of New York, his native State, had abolished slavery without a struggle or a groan. Great God, how independent! From henceforth slavery is tolerated where it exists, constitution or no constitution, people or no people, right or wrong: *Vox Matti*! *Vox Diaboli!* And peradventure, his great "sub-treasury" scheme was a piece of the same mind. But the man and his measures have such a striking resemblance to the anecdote of the Welshman and his cart-tongue, that when the Constitution was so long that is allowed slavery at the capitol of a free people, it could not be cut off; but when it was so short that it needed a *sub-treasury* to save the funds of the nation, it *could be spliced!* Oh, granny, granny, what a long tail our puss has got.* * * * But his mighty whisk through the great national fire, for the presidential chestnuts, *burnt the locks of his glory with the blaze of his folly!*

In the United States the people are the government, and their united voice is the only sovereign that should rule, the only power that should be obeyed, and the only gentlemen that should be honored at home and abroad, on the land and on the sea. Wherefore, were I the president of the United States, by the voice of a virtuous people, I would honor the old paths of the venerated fathers of freedom; I would walk in the tracks of the illustrious patriots who carried the ark of the Government upon their shoulders with an eye single to the glory of the people, and when that people petitioned to abolish slavery in the slave states, I would use all honorable means to have their prayers granted, and, give liberty to the captive by paying the Southern gentlemen a reasonable equivalent for his property, that the while nation might be free indeed!

When the people petitioned for a National Bank, I would use by best endeavors to have their prayers answered, and establish one on national principles to save taxes, and make them the controllers of its ways and means. And when the people petitioned to possess the territory of Oregon, or any other contiguous territory, I would lend the influence of a Chief Magistrate to grant so reasonable a request, that they might extend the mighty efforts and enterprise of a free people from the east to the west sea, and make the wilderness blossom as the rose. And when a neighboring realm petitioned to join the union of liberty's sons, my voice would be, *Come*—yea, come, Texas; come Mexico, come Canada; and come, all the world: let us be brethren, let us be one great family, and let there be a universal peace. Abolish the cruel custom of prisons (except certain cases), penitentiaries, court-martials for desertion; and let reason and friendship reign over the ruins of ignorance and barbarity; yea, I would, as the universal friend of man, open the prisons, open the eyes, open the ears, and open the hearts of all people, to behold and enjoy freedom—unadulterated freedom; and God who once cleansed the violence of the earth with a flood, whose Son laid down His life for the salvation of all His Father gave him out of the world, and who has promised that He will come and purify the world again with fire in the last days, should be supplicated by me for the good of all people. With the highest esteem, I am a friend of virtue and of the people,

JOSEPH SMITH,
NAUVOO, ILLINOIS, February 7, 1844.

Source: *History of the Church,* 6:197–209

Appendix C:
Conference Schedule for Electioneer Missionaries

(Conferences were held on Saturday and Sunday)

Quincy, Ill.	May 4–5
Princess Grove, Ill.	May 11–12
Ottowa, Ill.	May 18–19
Chicago, Ill.	May 25–26
Comstock, Kallamazoo County, Mich.	June 1–2
Pleasant Valley, Mich.	June 8–9
Frankland, Oakland County, Mich.	June 15–16
Kirtland, Ohio	June 22–23
G. A. Neal's, six miles west of Lockport, N.Y.	June 29–30
Batavia, N.Y.	July 6–7
Portage, Alleghany County, N.Y.	July 13–14
Hamilton, Madison, N.Y.	July 20–21
Oswego, N.Y.	June 29–30
Adams, Jefferson County, N.Y.	July 6–7
London, Caledonia County, N.Y.	June 15–16
Northfield, Washington Country, ten miles of Montpelier, at Lyman Houghton's, N.Y.	June 29–30
Fairfield, Essex County, at Elder Tracy's, N.Y.	July 13–14
Boston, Mass.	June 29–30
Salem, Mass.	July 6–7
New Bedford, Mass.	July 13–14
Peterboro, N.H.	July 13–14
Lowell, Mass.	July 27–28

Scarboro, Maine ....July 6–7
Vinal Haven, Maine ....July 13–14
Westfield, Mass. ....July 27–28
Farmington, Mass. ....Aug. 3–4
New Haven, Conn..Aug. 10–11
Canaan, Conn. ....Aug. 17–18
Norwalk, Conn. ....Aug. 24–25
New York City, N.Y..Aug. 17–18
Philadelphia, Pa.. Aug. 31–Sept. 1
Dresden, Weekly County, Tenn. ....May 25–26
Eagle Creek, Benton County, Tenn......................June 8–9
Dyer County, C. H..June 22–23
Rutherford County, C. H., Tenn.......................July 20–21
Lexington, Henderson County, Tenn...................Aug. 3–4
New Albany, Clinton County, Ky......................June 29–30
Alquina, Fayette County, Iowa............................June 1–2
Pleasant Garden, Iowa.....................................June 15–16
Fort Wayne, Iowa...June 29–30
Northfield, Boon County, Iowa........................July 13–14
Cincinnati, Ohio .... May 18–19
Pittsburgh, Pa...June 1–2
Leechburg, Pa... June 15–16
Running Water Branch, Noxuble County, Miss ... June 1–2
Tuscaloosa, Ala..June 22–23
Washington, D.C. ....……....Sept. 7–15

Source: *History of the Church*, 6:334–35.

Appendix D:
Electioneer Missionaries

(Those numbered "1st" and "2nd" take the presidency of the several states to which they are appointed.)

Maine

J. Butterfield, 1st; Jonathan H. Hale; Elbridge Tufts, 2nd; Henry Herriman; S. B. Stoddard; John Moon

New Hampshire

W. Snow, 1st; Harley Morley; Haward Egan, 2nd; Israel Barlow; Alvin Cooley; David Clough, Sen.; John S. Twiss; Calvin Reed; Charles A. Adams; Chilion Mack; Bethuel Miller; Isaac Burton; A. D. Boynton

Massachusetts

Daniel Spencer, 1st; George Lloyd; Milton F. Bartlett; Orlando D. Hovey; Daniel Loveland; Nathaniel Ashby; Joseph J. Woodbury; Samuel P. Hoyt; W. H. Woodbury; Daniel W. Gardner; John R. Blanchard

Rhode Island

William Seabury, 1st; Melvin Wilbur; Thomas McTaggart

Connecticut

E. H. Davis, 1st; Quartus S. Sparks

Vermont

Erastus Snow, 1st; Warren Snow; William Hyde; Dominicus Carter; Denman Cornish; Levi W. Hancock; Jeremiah Hatch; Alfred Cordon; Martin Titus; Charles Snow; William Haight; James C. Snow; John D. Chase; A. M. Harding; Josiah H. Perry; Isaac Houston; Amos Hodges

New York

C. W. Wandell, 1st; William Newland; Marcellus Bates, 2nd; Allen Wait; Truman Gillett; William H. Parshall; A. A. Farnham; C. H. Wheelock; Edmund Ellsworth; Timothy B. Foote; Gregory Bentley; George W. Fowler; Homer C. Hoyt; Henry L. Cook; Isaac Chase; William W. Dryer; Simeon A. Dunn; Elijah Reed; Daniel Shearer; Solon Foster; James W. Phippin; Hiram Bennett; J. H. Van Natta; Chandler Holbrook; Samuel P. Bacon; Lyman Hall; Bradford W. Elliott; William Felshaw; J. R. G. Phelps; Daniel Fisher; Joseph P. Noble; D. H. Redfield; John Tanner; Martin H. Tanner; Thomas Fuller; G. D. Goldsmith; O. M. Duel; Charles Thompson; Samuel White; B. C. Ellsworth; W. R. R. Stowell; Archibald Bates; William D. Pratt; David Pettigrew; Marcellus McKeown; Ellis Eames; Horace S. Eldredge

New Jersey

Ezra T. Benson, 1st; John Pack

Pennsylvania

D. D. Yearsley, 1st; Wm. P. McIntyre; Edson Whipple, 2nd; Jacob Zundall; John Duncan; Orrin D. Farlin; Stephen Post; Henry Mouer; G. W. Crouse; G. Chamberlain; Jacob Shoemaker; Thomas Hess; Stephen Winchester; A. J. Glaefke; Hyrum Nyman; Henry Dean; J. M. Cole; James Downing; Charles Warner

Delaware

John Jones; Jonathan O. Duke; Warren Snow; Justus Morse

Maryland

Jacob Hamblin; Patrick Norris; Lyman Stoddard

Virginia

B. Winchester, 1st; James Park; S. C. Shelton, 2nd; A. W. Whitney; Geo. D. Watt, 3rd; Pleasant Ewell; Chapman Duncan; W. E. Higginbottom; Joseph King; John F. Betts; Peter Fife; Alfred B. Lambson; Robert Hamilton; David Evans

North Carolina

A. McRae, 1st; John Holt; Aaron Razer, 2nd; John Houston; Thomas Guymon; James Sanderson; George Watt

South Carolina

Alonzo LeBaron, 1st; Ekells Truly; John M. Emell; William Smith; William D. Lyman

Georgia

Morgan L. Gardner; Miles Anderson; Isaac Beebe; S.E. Carpenter

Kentucky

John D. Lee, 1st; D. D. Hunt; D. H. Rogers; M. B. Welton; Samuel B. Frost; Horace B. Owens; John O. Angus; Joseph Holbrook; Charles Spry; Hiram W. Mikesell; John H. Reid; Garret W. Mikesell; William Watkins

Tennessee

A. O. Smoot, 1st; J. J. Castell; Alphonzo Young, 2nd; J. A.

Kelting; W. W. Riley; J. Hampton; Amos Davis; Alfred Bell; L. T. Coon; Armstead Moffitt; Jackson Smith; D. P. Rainey; W. P. Vance; James Holt; H. D. Buys; Warren Smith; A. D. Young; J. J. Sasnett; Joseph Younger; H. B. Jacobs; G. W. Langley; John L. Fullmer; G. Penn; Joseph Mount

Alabama

B. L. Clapp, 1st; L. D. Butler; G. W. Brandon; T. J. Brandon

Mississippi

J. B. Walker; Daniel Tyler; Ethan Barrus

Louisiana

J. B. Bosworth, 1st; John Kelly; H. H. Wilson; George Pew; Wm. Nelson; Lorenzo Moore

Arkansas

A. A. Simmons; J. A. McIntosh; Darwin Chase; Nathaniel Leavitt

Ohio

Lorenzo Snow, 1st; William Batson; L. Brooks, 2nd; G. C. Riser; Alfred Brown; Clark Lewis; J. J. Riser; B. W. Wilson; J. Carroll; A. W. Condit; L. O. Littlefield; Loren Babbitt; J. M. Powers; Elijah Newman; Milo Andrus; Milton Stow; John Lovelace; Edson Barney; W. H. Folsom; Hiram Dayton; John Cooper; Jacob Morris; S. Carter; Ezra Strong; John Nichols; J. M. Emmett; David Jones; Allen Tulley; Nathaniel Childs; P. H. Young; Jesse Johnson; S. P. Hutchins; J. A. Casper; J. H. Foster; Joseph Rose; Nathan T. Porter; W. Brothers; Ezra Vincent; Jared Porter; Lysander Dayton; John W. Roberts

Indiana

Amasa Lyman, 1st; U. V. Stewart; F. P. Dykes, 2nd; Washington Lemon; A. L. Lamoreaux; Edward Carlin; Charles Hopkins; L. D. Young; F. M. Edwards; Wm. Snow; Salmon Warner; Nathan Tanner; F. D. Richards; Wm. Martindale; S. W. Richards; Henry Elliott; John Mackey; A. F. Farr; James Newberry; John Jones; Abraham Palmer; Frederick Ott; John G. Smith

Michigan

Charles C. Rich, 1st; Wm. Savage; Harvey Green, 2nd; David Savage; Thomas Dunn; Graham Coltrin; R. C. Sprague; Samuel Parker; Joseph Curtis; Jeremiah Curtis; Zebedee Coltrin; C. W. Hubbard; Reuben W. Strong; S. D. Willard; L. N. Kendall; Wm. Gribble

Illinois

E. H. Groves, 1st; Morris Phelps, 2nd; John Vance S. Mulliner; H. Olmstead, Galena; John Gould; H. W. Barnes, do.; Zenus H. Gurley; Hiram Mott; Jefferson Hunt; David Candland; Jacob L. Burnham; W. A. Duncan; D. J. Kershner; Wm. O. Clark; N. Leavitt; Almon Bathrick; John Laurence; P. H. Buzzard; Nathan A. West; Zachariah Hardy; Levi Jackman; John Hammond; Abel Lamb; G. W. Hickerson; Howard Coray; Daniel Allen; Stephen Markham; David Judah; Levi Stewart; Thomas Dobson; James Graham; James Nelson; Timothy S. Hoit; David Lewis; Duncan McArthur

Missouri

A. H. Perkins, 1st; Wm. Coray; John Lowry, 2nd; O. M. Allen; Wm. G. Rule; Wm. H. Jordan

Wisconsin Territory

S. H. Briggs

Free

R. Nickerson, 1st; A. C. Nickerson; L. S. Nickerson

Source: *History of the Church*, 6:335–40

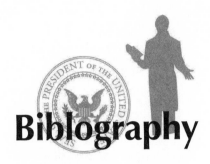

Bibliography

Allen, James B. "Was Joseph Smith a Serious Candidate for the Presidency". Ensign (September 1973): 21-22.

Allen, James B., and Glen M. Leonard. *The Story of the Latter-day Saints.* Salt Lake City: Deseret Book, 1992.

Andrus, Hyrum L. *Joseph Smith and World Government.* Salt Lake City: Deseret Book, 1958.

Baker, LeGrand L. *Murder of the Mormon Prophet: Political Prelude to the Death of Joseph Smith.* Salt Lake City: Eborn Books, 2006.

Alexander L. Baugh. "Extermination Order." In *Encyclopedia of Latter-day Saint History.* Edited by Arnold K. Garr, et al. Salt Lake City: Deseret Book, 2000. 351.

Church History in the Fulness of Times, Salt Lake City: The Church of Jesus Christ of Latter-day Saints, 2000. 286.

Clark, James R. "The Kingdom of God, the Council of Fifty, and the Star of Deseret." *Utah Historical Quarterly* 26 (April 1958): 130–48.

Durham, G. Homer. *Joseph Smith: Prophet-Statesman.* Salt Lake City: Bookcraft, 1944.

Ehat, Andrew R. "'It Seems Like Heaven Began on Earth': Joseph Smith and the Constitution of the Kingdom of God." *BYU Studies* 20 (Spring 1980): 253–79.

Garr, Arnold K. "General Smith's Views of the Powers and Policies of the Government of the United States." In *Encyclopedia of Latter-day Saint History*. Edited by Arnold K. Garr, et al. Salt Lake City: Deseret Book, 2000, 419–20.

———. "Joseph Smith: Candidate for President of the United States." In *Regional Studies in Latter-day Saint Church History: Illinois*. Edited by H. Dean Garrett. Provo, Utah: Department of Church History and Doctrine, Brigham Young University, 1995: 151-168.

———. "Joseph Smith for President: The Quorum of the Twelve Apostles in New England." In *Regional Studies in Latter-day Saint History: The New England States*. Provo, Utah: Religious Studies Center, Brigham Young University, 2004, 47-64.

———. "Joseph Smith: Mayor of Nauvoo." *Mormon Historical Studies* 3, no. 1 (Spring 2002): 29-46.

———. "Joseph Smith Meets President Van Buren." In *Joseph: Exploring the Life and Ministry of the Prophet*. Edited by Susan Easton Black and Andrew C. Skinner. Salt Lake City: Deseret Book, 2005.

———. "Presidential Campaign of Joseph Smith." In *Encyclopedia of Latter-day Saint History*. Edited by Arnold K. Garr, et al. Salt Lake City: Deseret Book, 2000, 944–45.

Godfrey, Kenneth W. "Council of Fifty." In *Encyclopedia of Mormonism*. 4 vols. Edited by Daniel H. Ludlow. New York: Macmillan, 1992, 1:326–27.

Hansen, Klaus J. *Quest for Empire: The Political Kingdom of God and The Council of Fifty in Mormon History*. Lincoln, Nebraska: University of Nebraska Press, 1974.

Hickman, Martin B. "The Political Legacy of Joseph Smith." *Dialogue: A Journal of Mormon Thought* (Autumn 1968): 22–27.

Jessee, Dean C. "Joseph Smith's 19 July 1840 Discourse." *BYU Studies* 19, no 3. (Spring): 1979, 390-394

———. *Papers of Joseph Smith.* 2 vols. Salt Lake City: Deseret Book, 1989–1992.

Johnson, Clark V., ed. *Mormon Redress Petitions.* Provo, Utah: Religious Studies Center, Brigham Young University, 1992.

Kimball, James L. "A Wall to Defend Zion: The Nauvoo Charter." *BYU Studies* 15, no. 4 (Summer 1975): 491-497.

Nauvoo City Council Minutes. LDS Church Archives, Family and Church History Department, The Church of Jesus Christ of Latter-day Saints, Salt Lake City.

The Personal Writings of Joseph Smith. Edited by Dean C. Jessee. Salt Lake City: Deseret Book, 1984.

Poll, Richard D. "Joseph Smith's Presidential Platform." *Dialogue: Journal of Mormon Thought* (Autumn 1968): 17–21.

Quinn, Michael D. "The Council of Fifty and Its Members, 1844 to 1945." *BYU Studies* 20 (Winter 1980): 163–97.

Roberts, B. H. *A Comprehensive History of The Church of Jesus Christ of Latter-day Saints.* 6 vols. Provo, Utah: Brigham Young University, 1965.

Robertson, Margaret C. "The Campaign and the Kingdom: The Activities of the Electioneers in Joseph Smith's Presidential Campaign." *BYU Studies* 39, no. 3 (2000): 147–80.

Shipps, Jan. "The Mormons in Politics, 1839–1844." Master's thesis, University of Colorado, 1962.

————. "The Mormons in Politics: The First Hundred Years." Ph.D. dissertation, University of Colorado, 1965.

Skinner, Andrew C. "John C. Bennett: For Prophet or Profit?" *Regional Studies in Latter-day Saint Church History: Illinois.* Provo, Utah: Department of Church History and Doctrine, Brigham Young University, 1995, 257–58.

Smith, Joseph. *History of the Church of Jesus Christ of Latter-day Saints.* 7 vols. Edited by B. H. Roberts. Salt Lake City: Deseret Book, 1965.

Thompson, Edward George. "A Study of the Political Involvements in the Career of Joseph Smith." Master's thesis, Brigham Young University, 1966.

Van Orden, Bruce A. "William W. Phelps's Service in Nauvoo as Joseph Smith's Political Clerk." *BYU Studies* 32 (Winter and Spring 1991): 81-94.

Wicks, Robert S., and Fred R. Foister. *Junius & Joseph: Presidential Politics and the Assassination of the First Mormon Prophet.* Logan, Utah: Utah State University Press, 2005.

Woodruff, Wilford. *Wilford Woodruff's Journal, 1833–1898.* 9 vols. Edited by Scott G. Kenney. Midvale, Utah: Signature Books, 1983.

Young, Brigham. *Manuscript History of Brigham Young.* Compiled by Elden Jay Watson. Salt Lake City: Smith Secretarial Service, 1968.

Endnotes

1. Thomas Carlyle, *Heroes and Hero Worship* (Chicago: Union School Finishing Co., 1900), 4.

2. See Arnold K. Garr, "Joseph Smith: Candidate for President of the United States," 151–68; Joseph Smith, "General Smith's Views of the Powers and Policies of the Government of the United States," 419–20; Arnold K. Garr, "Presidential Campaign of Joseph Smith," 944–45; Arnold K. Garr, "Joseph Smith: Mayor of Nauvoo," 29–46; Arnold K. Garr, "Joseph Smith for President: The Quorum of the Twelve Apostles in New England," 47–64; Arnold K. Garr, "Joseph Smith Meets President Van Buren," 340–48.

3. See Clark V. Johnson, ed., *Mormon Redress Petitions.* (Provo, Utah: Religious Studies Center, 1992).

4. Joseph Smith, *History of the Church,* 4:16, 18.

5. Smith, *History of the Church,* 4:80.

6. Smith, *History of the Church,* 6:64–65.

7. Smith, *History of the Church,* 6:188.

8. Smith, *History of the Church,* 6:210–11.

9. Smith, *History of the Church,* 6:189. In *History of the Church,* the Prophet sometimes calls the pamphlet *Views of the Powers and Policy of the Government of the United States.* However, when the pamphlet was published, it was officially titled *General Smith's Views of the Powers and Policy of the Government of the United States.*

10. Smith, *History of the Church,* 6:224.

11. Smith, *History of the Church,* 6:225–26.

12. B. H. Roberts, *A Comprehensive History of The Church of Jesus Christ of Latter-day Saints,* 2:207–8.

13. Smith, *History of the Church,* 6:390.

14. Smith, *History of the Church,* 6:188, 334.

15. James B. Allen and Glen M. Leonard, *The Story of the Latter-day Saints*, 201.

16. Kenneth W. Godfrey, "Council of Fifty," 1:326.

17. Allen and Leonard, *The Story of the Latter-day Saints*, 204.

18. Smith, *History of the Church*, 6:325.

19. Smith, *History of the Church*, 6:335–40.

20. Smith, *History of the Church*, 6:335–40.

21. *Times and Seasons* 5 (15 April 1844): 504–6.

22. Smith, *History of the Church*, 6:334–35.

23. Robert S. Wicks and Fred R. Foister, *Junius & Joseph: Presidential Politics and the Assassination of the First Mormon Prophet*, 108. This page features a map that indicates the location of the cities where newspapers published *General Smith's Views*.

24. Roberts, *Comprehensive History of the Church*, 205; see also LeGrand L. Baker, *Murder of the Mormon Prophet*, 186–209. Here, Baker reprints and discusses several articles concerning *General Smith's Views* that appeared in newspapers in the United States.

25. Smith, *History of the Church*, 5:526.

26. Smith, *History of the Church*, 6:188.

27. Smith, *History of the Church*, 6:210–11.

28. Roberts, *Comprehensive History of the Church*, 2:208–9.

29. Smith, *History of the Church*, 6:243.

30. James B. Allen, "Was Joseph Smith a Serious Candidate for the Presidency?" *Ensign*, September 1973, 21.

31. Allen, "Was Joseph Smith a Serious Candidate for the Presidency?" 22.

32. Allen, "Was Joseph Smith a Serious Candidate for the Presidency?" 22.

33. Durham, *Joseph Smith: Prophet-Statesman*, 203.

34. Smith, *History of the Church*, 3:175.

35. The extermination order was rescinded in 1976 (see Conference Report, October 1976, 4–5).

36. Smith, *History of the Church*, 3:175.

37. Alexander L. Baugh, "Extermination Order," 351.

38. Estimates of the number of Mormons living in Missouri in 1838–39 vary from 5,500 to 15,000. Joseph Smith, Sidney Rigdon, and Elias Higbee wrote of 15,000 (see Johnson, ed., *Mormon Redress Petitions*, 116). B. H. Roberts used a figure of 12,000–15,000 (see *Comprehensive History of The Church of Jesus Christ of Latter-day Saints*, 1:511). Allen and Leonard

also used 12,000–15,000 (see *The Story of the Latter-day Saints*, 134). Hyrum Smith claimed that there were 12,000–14,000 (see Smith, *History of the Church*, 3:424). Andrew Jensen wrote of 12,000 in Caldwell and Davies Counties (see *Encyclopedic History of The Church of Jesus Christ of Latter-day Saints* [Salt Lake City: Deseret News, 1941), 107). Parley P. Pratt said there were "10 or 11 thousand souls" (Johnson, *Mormon Redress Petitions*, 95). William G. Hartley used a figure of 10,000–12,000 (see "Missouri's 1838 Extermination Order and the Mormons' Forced Removal to Illinois," in *A City of Refuge: Quincy Illinois*, ed. Susan Easton Black and Richard E. Bennett [Riverton, Utah: Millennial Press, 2000], 6). *Church History in the Fulness* of Times (Salt Lake City: The Church of Jesus Christ of Latter-day Saints, 1989) uses 8,000–10,000 (see page 215). Leonard said at least 8,000 (see *Nauvoo: A Place of Peace, A People of Promise* [Salt Lake City: Deseret Book, 2002], 31). Alexander L. Baugh estimates 5,500–8,000 (see "Mormon Population Figures in Northern Missouri in 1839" [an unpublished paper in the possession of the author; used by permission] 3).

39. See Johnson, ed., *Mormon Redress Petitions.*
40. Smith, *History of the Church*, 4:16, 18.
41. Smith, *History of the Church*, 4:19.
42. Roberts, *Comprehensive History of the Church*, 2:29.
43. *The Papers of Martin Van Buren*, ed. Lucy Fish West (Alexandria, Va.: Chadwick—Healey Inc., 1989), microfilm of Van Buren's papers in Library of Congress, reel 33, Harold B. Lee Library, Brigham Young University. This was a letter from Judge Adams to Martin Van Buren, written in Springfield, Illinois, on November 9, 1839.
44. Dean C. Jessee, ed., *The Personal Writings of Joseph Smith*, 448; spelling and punctuation standardized.
45. Smith, *History of the Church*, 4:21.
46. Smith, *History of the Church*, 4:23–24.
47. Smith, *History of the Church*, 4:39–40.
48. Smith, *History of the Church*, 4:39–40.
49. Smith, *History of the Church*, 4:39–40.
50. Smith, *History of the Church*, 4:42.
51. Smith, *History of the Church*, 4:43–44.
52. Smith, *History of the Church*, 4:38.
53. Roberts, *Comprehensive History of the Church*, 2:32.
54. Smith, *History of the Church*, 4:44.

55.   Smith, *History of the Church*, 4:74.
56.   Smith, *History of the Church*, 4:47.
57.   Parley P. Pratt, *Autobiography of Parley P. Pratt* (Salt Lake City: Deseret Book, 1973) 297.
58.   Pratt, *Autobiography,* 298–99.
59.   Smith, *History of the Church*, 4:77.
60.   Smith, *History of the Church*, 4:79.
61.   Some histories maintain that Joseph Smith's interview with Martin Van Buren on November 29, 1839, was the only one he had with the president (see *Church History in the Fulness of Times*, 221; see also Roberts, *Comprehensive History of the Church*, 2:30.) However, the *History of the Church* has an entry on February 6, 1840, about the Prophet visiting Van Buren. Historians disagree over whether this entry is simply a retelling of the visit on November 29, 1839, or the recording of a second visit on February 6, 1840. Evidence favors two distinct visits. In the November account the Prophet said that Van Buren "felt to sympathize" with the Mormons. In contrast, in the February account, the Prophet calls Van Buren "insolent" and not worthy to be president. In this account Joseph Smith also said that he planned to leave Washington, D.C., "in but a few days." If Joseph would have departed in a few days after his visit in November, he would not have been in Washington, D.C., in February. The *History of the Church* makes clear that the Prophet was definitely in Washington, D.C., in February.
62.   Smith, *History of the Church*, 4:80.
63.   Smith, *History of the Church*, 4:80. On February 6, Joseph Smith stated that he "stayed but a few days" before he left Washington, D.C. However, he might have stayed as late as February 20. On that day he wrote, "Judge Higbee I left at Washington, and he wrote me as follows." Higbee's letter was dated February 20.
64.   Smith, *History of the Church*, 4:89.
65.   See Smith, *History of the Church*, 4:81, 83, 85, 88, 94, 98.
66.   Smith, *History of the Church*, 4:90–92.
67.   Smith, *History of the Church*, 4:98–99.
68.   Dean C. Jessee, "Joseph Smith's 19 July 1840 Discourse," *BYU Studies* 19, no. 3 (Spring 1979): 392.
69.   Smith, *History of the Church*, 4:205.
70.   Smith, *History of the Church*, 4:205.
71.   Smith, *History of the Church*, 4:206.
72.   James L. Kimball Jr., "A Wall to Defend Zion," 492.

73. Smith, *History of the Church*, 4:249. Andrew F. Smith claims that "it is unlikely that this was an accurate reflection of what really happened." Smith gives Bennett more credit, saying, "He was an experienced and accomplished lobbyist, having written and passed bills in Ohio, Virginia, Indiana, and Illinois" (see Andrew F. Smith, *The Saintly Scoundrel: The Life and Time of Dr. John Cook Bennett* (Urbana and Chicago: University of Illinois Press, 1997), 60.

74. *Times and Seasons*, 2 (1 January 1841): 266–67.

75. Smith, *History of the Church*, 4:240.

76. Smith, *History of the Church*, 4:241.

77. Smith, *History of the Church*, 4:242.

78. Smith, *History of the Church*, 4:243.

79. Smith, *History of the Church*, 4:244.

80. *Times and Seasons* 2 (1 January 1841): 264.

81. *Times and Seasons* 2 (1 January 1841): 266–67.

82. Kimball, "A Wall to Defend Zion," 496.

83. Kimball, "A Wall to Defend Zion," 496.

84. Smith, *History of the Church*, 4:287.

85. See James B. Allen, et al., *Men with a Mission, 1837–1841: The Quorum of the Twelve Apostles in the British Isles* (Salt Lake City: Deseret Book, 1992).

86. Nauvoo City Council Minutes, 22 February 1841 and 1 March 1841, typescript, 3, 8, 15, LDS Church Archives, Family and Church History Department, The Church of Jesus Christ of Latter-day Saints, Salt Lake City.

87. Nauvoo City Council Minutes, 3 February 1841; see also Smith, *History of the Church*, 4:288–94. The *History of the Church* has these events in a different sequence than they appear in the Nauvoo City Council Minutes. Here the sequence is as it appears in the minutes.

88. Smith, *History of the Church*, 4:295.

89. Smith, *History of the Church*, 4:295–96.

90. Nauvoo City Council Minutes, 15 February 1841; see also Smith, *History of the Church*, 4:299.

91. Nauvoo City Council Minutes, 1 March 1841; see also Smith, *History of the Church*, 4:306.

92. Allen, *Men with a Mission*, 304–6; see also Smith, *History of the Church*, 4:414.

93. Nauvoo City Council Minutes, 4 September 1841; see also Smith, *History of the Church*, 4:414.

94. Nauvoo City Council Minutes, 23 October 1841.

95.   Nauvoo City Council Minutes, 30 October 1841; see also Smith, *History of the Church,* 4:442.

96.   *Times and Seasons* 3 (1 February 1842): 683–84, 686. The *History of the Church* refers to the office as "mayor, pro tem" (4:501).

97.   *Times and Seasons* 3 (1 February 1842): 683–84.

98.   Nauvoo City Council Minutes, 22 January 1842.

99.   Smith, *History of the Church,* 4:341.

100. Andrew C. Skinner, "John C. Bennett: For Prophet or Profit?" in *Regional Studies in Latter-day Saint Church History: Illinois,* (Provo, Utah: Department of Church History and Doctrine, Brigham Young University, 1995), 257–58.

101. Skinner, "John C. Bennett," 257.

102. Smith, *History of the Church,* 5:4.

103. Skinner, "John C. Bennett," 258.

104. Smith, *History of the Church,* 5:11–12.

105. *Times and Seasons* 3 (1 August 1842): 870–71.

106. Smith, *History of the Church,* 5:12–13.

107. Nauvoo City Council Minutes, 19 May 1842.

108. Smith, *History of the Church,* 5:13.

109. Jessee, *Papers of Joseph Smith,* 2:384; see also Smith, *History of the Church,* 5:12.

110. Jessee, *Papers of Joseph Smith,* 2:384; see also Smith, *History of the Church,* 5:12.

111. Jessee, *Papers of Joseph Smith,* 2:384; see also Smith, *History of the Church,* 5:12–13.

112. Jessee, *Papers of Joseph Smith,* 2:385; see also Smith, *History of the Church,* 5:13.

113. Nauvoo City Council Minutes, 19 May 1842.

114. Jessee, *Papers of Joseph Smith,* 2:386; see also Smith, *History of the Church,* 5:14–15.

115. Smith, *History of the Church,* 5:15.

116. Jessee, *Papers of Joseph Smith,* 2:386.

117. Nauvoo City Council Minutes, 5 July 1842; see also Smith, *History of the Church,* 5:57.

118. Roberts, *Comprehensive History of the Church,* 2:149.

119. Roberts, *Comprehensive History of the Church,* 2:149.

120. Jessee, *Papers of Joseph Smith,* 2:402–3; see also Smith, *History of the Church,* 5:86–87.

121. Jessee, *Papers of Joseph Smith,* 2:408; see also Smith, *History of the Church,* 5:93. Wilson Law had replaced John C. Bennett as major general of the Nauvoo Legion (see Roberts, *Comprehensive*

History of the Church, 2:153).

122. Roberts, *Comprehensive History of the Church,* 2:153–54; see also Jessee, *Papers of Joseph Smith,* 2:485; Smith, *History of the Church,* 5:167.

123. Roberts, *Comprehensive History of the Church,* 2:155–56.

124. Jessee, *Papers of Joseph Smith,* 2:504–5; see also Smith, *History of the Church,* 5:205–6; Roberts, *Comprehensive History of the Church,* 2:156.

125. Roberts states that William Law arrested Joseph Smith (see Roberts, *Comprehensive History of the Church,* 2:156), but the Prophet's published history states that Wilson Law arrested the Prophet (see Smith, *History of the Church,* 5:209).

126. Roberts, *Comprehensive History of the Church,* 2:156–58; see also Smith, *History of the Church,* 5:223–31.

127. Smith, *History of the Church,* 5:248–49.

128. Smith, *History of the Church,* 5:252.

129. Smith, *History of the Church,* 5:264–65.

130. Smith, *History of the Church,* 5:286.

131. Roberts, *Comprehensive History of the Church,* 2:180.

132. Smith, *History of the Church,* 5:295.

133. Smith, *History of the Church,* 5:298.

134. Smith, *History of the Church,* 6:103; see also Roberts, *Comprehensive History of the Church,* 2:198–99.

135. Smith, *History of the Church,* 6:103–4.

136. Nauvoo City Council Minutes, 8 December 1843; see also Smith, *History of the Church,* 6:105.

137. Nauvoo City Council Minutes, 21 December 1843; see also Smith, *History of the Church,* 6:131.

138. Nauvoo City Council Minutes, 21 December 1843; see also Smith, *History of the Church,* 6:124. *The Story of the Latter-day Saints,* page 198, incorrectly states that the council authorized Orson Hyde to be the delegate.

139. Smith, *History of the Church,* 6:149.

140. Nauvoo City Council Minutes, 29 December 1843; see also Smith, *History of the Church,* 6:153.

141. *Times and Seasons* 4 (October 1, 1843): 334.

142. Smith, *History of the Church,* 6:64-65.

143. Smith, *History of the Church,* 6:65.

144. Smith, *History of the Church,* 6:156; emphasis added.

145. Smith, *History of the Church,* 6:159–60; emphasis added.

146. Smith, *History of the Church,* 6:188.

147. Smith, *History of the Church,* 6:189. In *History of the Church,* the

Prophet sometimes calls the pamphlet *Views of the Powers and Policy of the Government of the United States*. However, when the pamphlet was published, it was officially titled *General Smith's Views of the Powers and Policy of the Government of the United States*.

148. Bruce A. Van Orden, "William W. Phelps's Service in Nauvoo as Joseph Smith's Political Clerk," *BYU Studies* 32 (Winter and Spring 1991): 94 n.

149. Smith, *History of the Church*, 6:75 n.

150. Smith, *History of the Church*, 6:75 n.

151. Jessee, *The Papers of Joseph Smith*, 1:xxiv.

152. Smith, *History of the Church*, 6:189.

153. Smith, *History of the Church*, 6:197.

154. Smith, *History of the Church*, 6:197; emphasis added.

155. Smith, *History of the Church*, 5:526.

156. *Church History in the Fulness of Times*, 269–70.

157. Martin B. Hickman, "The Political Legacy of Joseph Smith," *Dialogue* (August 1968): 23.

158. Smith, *History of the Church*, 6:65.

159. Smith, *History of the Church*, 6:156.

160. Smith, *History of the Church*, 6:210–11; emphasis added.

161. Smith, *History of the Church*, 6:206.

162. Smith, *History of the Church*, 6:206.

163. Joseph Fielding Smith, comp., *Teachings of the Prophet Joseph Smith* (Salt Lake City: Deseret Book, 1963), 327.

164. Smith, *History of the Church*, 6:205.

165. *The New Encyclopedia Britannica*, 30 vols. (Chicago: William Benton, 1974), 4:681.

166. George Brown Tindall, *America: A Narrative History*, 2 vols. (New York: W. W. Norton & Company, 1988), 1:697.

167. Smith, *History of the Church*, 6:204–5.

168. U.S. Bureau of the Census, *Historical Statistics of the United States, 1789–1945* (Washington, D.C.: Government Printing Office, 1949), 294.

169. Smith, *History of the Church*, 6:205.

170. Smith, *History of the Church*, 6:205.

171. Ernest Sutherland Bates, *The Story of Congress, 1789–1935* (New York: Harper, 1936), 101.

172. Smith, *History of the Church*, 6:205.

173. Smith, *History of the Church*, 6:205.

174. Smith, *History of the Church*, 6:205.

175. Smith, *History of the Church*, 6:205.

176. Smith, *History of the Church,* 6:197.
177. Smith, *History of the Church,* 6:206.
178. Milton V. Backman Jr., *The Heavens Resound* (Salt Lake City: Deseret Book, 1983), 314–20.
179. Smith, *History of the Church,* 6:206.
180. Smith, *History of the Church,* 6:206.
181. John A. Widtsoe, *Joseph Smith—Seeker after Truth* (Salt Lake City: Bookcraft, 1991), 219.
182. Smith, *History of the Church,* 6:210–11.
183. Smith, *History of the Church,* 6:224.
184. Smith, *History of the Church,* 6:225–26.
185. Wicks and Foister, *Junius & Joseph,* 108.
186. Roberts, *Comprehensive History of the Church,* 205. See also Baker, *Murder of the Mormon Prophet,* 186–209.
187. Smith, *History of the Church,* 6:260–61.
188. Allen and Leonard, *The Story of the Latter-day Saints,* 201–2.
189. Klaus J. Hansen, *Quest for Empire: The Political Kingdom of God and The Council of Fifty in Mormon History* (Lincoln, Neb.: University of Nebraska Press, 1974), 223.
190. Godfrey, "Council of Fifty," 1:326.
191. Allen and Leonard, *The Story of the Latter-day Saints,* 204.
192. For more on the Council of Fifty and the political kingdom of God, see Hyrum L. Andrus, *Joseph Smith and World Government;* see also James R. Clark, "The Kingdom of God, the Council of Fifty, and the Star of Deseret," *Utah Historical Quarterly* 26 (April 1958): 130–48; Andrew R. Ehat, "It Seems Like Heaven Began on Earth," 253–79; Klaus H. Hansen, *Quest for Empire;* Michael D. Quinn, "The Council of Fifty and Its Members, 1844 to 1945," 163–97.
193. Smith, *History of the Church,* 6:188.
194. Smith, *History of the Church,* 6:324.
195. Smith, *History of the Church,* 6:322.
196. Smith, *History of the Church,* 6:325.
197. Smith, *History of the Church,* 6:325.
198. Smith, *History of the Church,* 6:335–40.
199. *2007 Church Almanac* (Salt Lake City: *Deseret Morning News,* 2006), 637.
200. *2007 Church Almanac,* 637.
201. Smith, *History of the Church,* 6:335–40.
202. *Times and Seasons* 5 (15 April 1844): 504–6.
203. Smith, *History of the Church,* 6:334–35.
204. *Times and Seasons* 5 (15 April 1844): 506.

205. *Times and Seasons* 5 (15 April 1844): 506.
206. *Times and Seasons* 5 (15 April 1844): 506.
207. Smith, *History of the Church*, 6:361.
208. Smith, *History of the Church*, 6:386, 389–92.
209. Wilford Woodruff, *Wilford Woodruff's Journal*, 2:394.
210. Woodruff, *Journal*, 2:394.
211. Woodruff, *Journal*, 2:397.
212. Woodruff, *Journal*, 2:398.
213. Woodruff, *Journal*, 2:400.
214. Woodruff, *Journal*, 2:400.
215. Woodruff, *Journal*, 2:400.
216. Woodruff, *Journal*, 2:402.
217. Woodruff, *Journal*, 2:403–4.
218. Woodruff, *Journal*, 2:405.
219. Woodruff, *Journal*, 2:406.
220. Woodruff, *Journal*, 2:406–9.
221. Woodruff, *Journal*, 2:410.
222. Woodruff, *Journal*, 2:411–12.
223. Woodruff, *Journal*, 2:412–13.
224. Smith, *History of the Church*, 7:136.
225. Smith, *History of the Church*, 7:136.
226. Smith, *History of the Church*, 7:136.
227. Smith, *History of the Church*, 7:136.
228. Smith, *History of the Church*, 7:136.
229. Smith, *History of the Church*, 7:136.
230. Smith, *History of the Church*, 7:136.
231. Smith, *History of the Church*, 7:137.
232. Brigham Young, *Manuscript History of Brigham Young*, 167; see also Smith, *History of the Church*, 7:136.
233. Smith, *History of the Church*, 7:136.
234. Smith, *History of the Church*, 7:137.
235. Smith, *History of the Church*, 7:137.
236. Smith, *History of the Church*, 7:137.
237. Young, *Manuscript History*, 167–68.
238. Young, *Manuscript History*, 168.
239. Young, *Manuscript History*, 168.
240. Young, *Manuscript History*, 168–69.
241. The publishers were William Law, Wilson Law, Charles Ivans, Frances M. Higbee, Chauncey L. Higbee, Robert D. Foster, and Charles A. Foster (see Smith, *History of the Church*, 6:444).
242. *Nauvoo Expositor*, 7 June 1844; photocopy in possession of author.

243. Nauvoo City Council Minutes, 10 June 1844, 3, 8, 15; see also Smith, *History of the Church*, 6:448.
244. Smith, *History of the Church*, 6:432.
245. *Warsaw Signal*, 12 June 1844, 2; cited in Roberts, *Comprehensive History of the Church*, 2:236.
246. Smith, *History of the Church*, 6:497.
247. Smith, *History of the Church*, 6:519.
248. *Millennial Star* 26 (28 May 1864): 343.
249. Woodruff, *Journal*, 2:414.
250. Woodruff, *Journal*, 2:414.
251. Smith, *History of the Church*, 6:386.
252. Smith, *History of the Church*, 6:386–97.
253. LaMar C. Berrett, ed., *Sacred Places: New England and Canada* (Salt Lake City: Bookcraft, 1999), 5.
254. Woodruff, *Journal*, 2:415.
255. Woodruff, *Journal*, 2:415.
256. Woodruff, *Journal*, 2:415.
257. Woodruff, *Journal*, 2:415.
258. Smith, *History of the Church*, 7:210.
259. Woodruff, *Journal*, 2:416.
260. Woodruff, *Journal*, 2:416.
261. Smith, *History of the Church*, 7:210.
262. Woodruff, *Journal*, 2:415.
263. Young, *Manuscript History*, 170.
264. Woodruff, *Journal*, 2:416.
265. Smith, *History of the Church*, 7:159.
266. Woodruff, *Journal*, 2:416, 417.
267. Young, *Manuscript History*, 170.
268. Smith, *History of the Church*, 7:169; see also Young, *Manuscript History*, 170.
269. Smith, *History of the Church*, 7:175.
270. Woodruff, *Journal*, 2:419–20.
271. Woodruff, *Journal*, 2:422.
272. Young, *Manuscript History*, 171.
273. Woodruff, *Journal*, 2:423.
274. Smith, *History of the Church*, 7:198.
275. Smith, *History of the Church*, 7:197–98.
276. Margaret C. Robertson, "The Campaign and the Kingdom," 149.
277. See Allen and Leonard, *The Story of the Latter-day Saints*, 139–40, 160–64; *Church History in the Fulness of Times*, 141–52, 211–13, 255–39; Allen, *Men with a Mission*.

278. *Church History in the Fulness of Times* (Salt Lake City: The Church of Jesus Christ of Latter-day Saints, 2000), 286.

279. Roberts, *Comprehensive History of the Church*, 2:208–9.

280. Smith, *History of the Church*, 6:243.

281. Smith, *History of the Church*, 6:188.

282. Smith, *History of the Church*, 6:210–11.

283. Smith, *History of the Church*, 6:605–6.

284. Smith, *History of the Church*, 6:606.

285. Smith, *History of the Church*, 6:606.

286. See Baker, *Murder of the Mormon Prophet;* see also Wicks and Foister, *Junius and Joseph.*

287. Allen, "Was Joseph Smith a Serious Candidate for the Presidency?" 21.

288. Allen, "Was Joseph Smith a Serious Candidate for the Presidency?" 22.

289. Smith, *History of the Church*, 6:188.

290. Smith, *History of the Church*, 6:231.

291. Smith, *History of the Church*, 6:232.

292. Smith, *History of the Church*, 6:322.

293. Smith, *History of the Church*, 6:324.

294. Smith, *History of the Church*, 6:325.

295. Smith, *History of the Church*, 6:400.

296. Ezra Taft Benson, *Teachings of Ezra Taft Benson* (Salt Lake City: Bookcraft, 1988), 676.

297. Benson, *Teachings of Ezra Taft Benson*, 676–77.

298. Crockford's was a famous gaming club house at no. 50 on the west side of St. James Street, London.

Author's Biographical Information

Arnold K. Garr is currently Department Chair and Professor of Church History and Doctrine at Brigham Young University where he has taught since 1991. Before teaching at BYU he was employed by the Church Educational System for 21 years in Utah, New York, Florida and Colorado. During the 1996-97 academic year, Brother Garr taught at the BYU Jerusalem Center for Near Eastern Studies.

He was born and raised in Ogden, Utah. He received a bachelor's degree from Weber State College, and a master's degree from Utah State University, both in history. He also earned a Ph.D. in American History with a minor in LDS Church History from Brigham Young University.

He is editor of *Encyclopedia of Latter-day Saint History* and author of *Christopher Columbus: A Latter-day Saint Perspective*. He has also published numerous articles pertaining to LDS Church History, including six on the political activities of Joseph Smith.

Brother Garr is currently a member of the Church Correlation, Materials Evaluation Committee. He has also served as a stake president's counselor, high councilor, bishop and branch president. As a young man, he served a mission in Finland.

He became a running enthusiast late in his life and has run five marathons since he turned sixty years old. He is married to the former Miss Cherie Burns, from Ogden, Utah, and they are the parents of five children.

SETTING THE RECORD STRAIGHT SERIES

MORMONS & MASONS

GILBERT W. SCHARFFS, Ph.D.

MORMONS POLYGAMY

JESSIE L. EMBRY

BLACKS & THE MORMON PRIESTHOOD

MARCUS H. MARTINS, Ph.D.

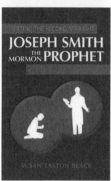

JOSEPH SMITH THE MORMON PROPHET

SUSAN EASTON BLACK

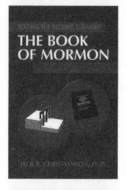

THE BOOK OF MORMON

JACK R. CHRISTIANSON, Ph.D.

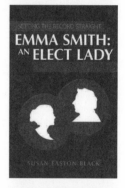

EMMA SMITH: AN ELECT LADY

SUSAN EASTON BLACK

MORMON TEMPLES

DEAN L. LARSEN

THE WORD OF WISDOM

STEVEN C. HARPER, Ph.D.

JOSEPH SMITH: PRESIDENTIAL CANDIDATE

ARNOLD K. GARR, Ph.D.